ROYAL ADMINISTRATION
AND NATIONAL RELIGION
IN ANCIENT PALESTINE

STUDIES IN THE HISTORY
OF THE
ANCIENT NEAR EAST

EDITED BY

M.H.E. WEIPPERT

VOLUME I

LEIDEN
E.J. BRILL
1982

ROYAL ADMINISTRATION AND NATIONAL RELIGION IN ANCIENT PALESTINE

BY

G.W. AHLSTRÖM

LEIDEN
E.J. BRILL
1982

Ahlström, G.W. – Royal administration and
national religion in ancient Palestine / by G.W.
Ahlström. – Leiden: Brill. – (Studies in the history
of the ancient Near East; vol. 1)

UDC 932(5-011)

ISBN 90 04 06562 8

PRINTED IN THE NETHERLANDS

To
Pernille
and
Hans

CONTENTS

FOREWORD

The intimate relationship between state and religion has been the purpose of this investigation. The religions of the ancient Near East have too often been looked upon from the viewpoints of modern man who is unable to comprehend that private religions had little place in these oriental societies. Religion was an expression of the life of a community, and therefore constituted a part of the political system, the basic premise being that of the god as the ruler of the nation.

This inquiry has grown out of a paper, "Sanctuaries and Royal Administration," which was delivered as a presidential address at the joint annual meetings of the Mid-West section of the Society of Biblical Literature and the Middle West Branch of the American Oriental Society, Bloomington, Indiana, on Febr. 27, 1978. It is quite natural that certain problems of compositional nature have arisen and it is only to be hoped that the reader be indulgent towards those which have not been perfectly solved.

I wish to express my gratitude to my colleague Professor Edward F. Wente for his many valuable comments and to Mrs. Beth Glazier-McDonald, M.A., to whom I am especially indebted. She has assisted me with the problems of composition and with rewriting the manuscript as well as with stylistically improving my English. Without her generous help this book would never have been published.

Chicago in May 1980   G.W. Ahlström

ACKNOWLEDGMENT

Special thanks should be expressed to Professor Manfred Weippert for accepting this opus in the new series of *Studies in the History of the Ancient Near East*. I also wish to express my gratefulness for his thorough reading of the manuscript and for his many valuable comments.

Chicago in September 1981.

GWA

ABBREVIATIONS

AASOR	The Annual of the American Schools of Oriental Research
ADAJ	Annual of the Department of Antiquities, Jordan
AfO	Archiv für Orientforschung
AJA	American Journal of Archaeology
AJSL	American Journal of Semitic Languages
ANET	Ancient Near Eastern Texts (ed. by J.B. Pritchard)
AOAT	Alter Orient und Altes Testament
AOS	American Oriental Series
ARAB	Ancient Records of Assyria and Babylonia (ed. by D.D. Luckenbill)
ARM	Archives Royales de Mari
ARW	Archiv für Religionswissenschaft
BA	Biblical Archaeologist
BASOR	Bulletin of the American Schools of Oriental Research
BJRL	Bulletin of the John Rylands Library
BK	Biblischer Kommentar (Altes Testament)
BWANT	Beiträge zur Wissenschaft vom Alten und Neuen Testament
BZAW	Beiheft zur Zeitschrift für die alttestamentliche Wissenschaft
CAD	The Assyrian Dictionary of the University of Chicago
CAH	Cambridge Ancient History
CHM	Cahiers histoire mondiale
EAEHL	Encyclopedia of Archaeological Excavations in the Holy Land
FRLANT	Forschungen zur Religion und Literatur des Alten und Neuen Testaments
HAT	Handbuch zum Alten Testament (ed. by O. Eissfeldt)
HTR	Harvard Theological Review
ICC	The International Critical Commentary of the Holy Scriptures of the Old and New Testament
IDB	Interpreter's Dictionary of the Bible
IEJ	Israel Exploration Journal
JAOS	Journal of the American Oriental Society
JBL	Journal of Biblical Literature
JCS	Journal of Cuneiform Studies
JEA	Journal of Egyptian Archaeology
JESHO	Journal of the Economic and Social History of the Orient
JNES	Journal of Near Eastern Studies
JQR	The Jewish Quarterly Review
JSS	Journal of Semitic Studies
KAI	Kanaanäische und Aramäische Inschriften (ed. by H. Donner and W. Röllig)
KS	A. Alt, Kleine Schriften
OIP	Oriental Institute Publications
PEQ	Palestine Exploration Quarterly
RA	Revue d'assyriologie et d'archéologie orientale
RAI	Recontre assyriologique internationale
RB	Revue biblique internationale
SAOC	Studies in Ancient Oriental Civilizations
SEÅ	Svensk Exegetisk Årsbok

SVT	Supplements to Vetus Testamentum
ThWAT	Theologisches Wörterbuch zum Alten Testament
ThZ	Theologische Zeitschrift
UF	Ugarit Forschungen
VAB	Vorderasiatische Bibliothek
VT	Vetus Testamentum
WMANT	Wissenschaftliche Monographien zum Alten und Neuen Testament
ZAW	Zeitschrift für die alttestamentliche Wissenschaft
ZDPV	Zeitschrift des deutschen Palästina-Vereins
ZfA	Zeitschrift für Assyriologie
ZThK	Zeitschrift für Theologie und Kirche

CHAPTER ONE

THE NATION AS THE GOD'S TERRITORY

The City

The phenomenon of urbanization is usually regarded as a process whose evolution is limited to a certain period or periods, the onset of which varied from one area to another. While this view may be correct if one takes into account solely the beginning of the process, there is, nevertheless, another aspect to be considered. With the rise of nations that were geographically more dispersed than city-states, the founding of new cities was often part of royal defense and administrative policy. "Forced urbanization of outlying sections resulted in a pacification of the country" by enabling pressure to be exerted upon unstable population elements and by securing the trade routes.[1] For instance, Assyrian kings "constantly founded new cities and peopled them with prisoners of war."[2] Moreover, new cities could also be built in order to 'replace' already existing ones that opposed the royal policy. Such was the case, for example, in Mesopotamia where there was a class of privileged cities (thought of as having divine protection) which were tax-exempt and whose people could not be used for the corvée.[3] From this perspective, the process of urbanization can be understood as both a political tool and as an ongoing process.

The Kings as builder

Building a city entailed not only the construction of houses, workshops, streets, and walls, but also water conduits, cisterns,[4] etc., and in Mesopotamia, for instance, canals. In the case of administrative centers it was neces-

---

[1] A.L. Oppenheim, *Ancient Mesopotamia. Portrait of a Dead Civilization,* Chicago and London 1964, p. 118, cf. J. Pedersen, *Israel* III-IV, London and Copenhagen (1940) 1953, p. 64.

[2] Oppenheim, "A Bird's-Eye View of Mesopotamian Economic History", in *Trade and Market in the Early Empires,* ed. by K. Polanyi, C.M. Arensberg, H.W. Pearson, New York and London (1957) 1965, p. 36.

[3] For this as a legal status, the so called *kidinnūtu* status, see Oppenheim, in *City Invincible,* ed. by C.H. Kraeling and R.M. Adams, Chicago 1960, pp. 81, 175, *id. Ancient Mesopotamia,* pp. 120 ff., cf. also H. Vanstiphout, "Political Ideology in Early Sumer", *Orientalia Lovaniensia Periodica* I, 1970, p. 9.

[4] Cf. 2 Kings 20:20, 2 Chr. 26:10. See also R. Miller, "Water Use in Syria and Palestine from the Neolithic to the Bronze Age", *World Archaeology,* 11/80, pp. 331–339.

sary to build a house for the prefect or governor and a house for the god, i.e.
a temple. These two buildings were the physical expressions of the national
government representing king and god. Temples built by the king were state
administrative places which often became the financial centers and the large
land holders of the country [5] (incidentally, this may solve the problem of
why the Levites received no "inheritance" in the land of Canaan). This is
the political reality behind the idea of the king as temple builder. [6] By con-
structing cities and temples the king acted as the protector and organizer of
the country and its people. He was, in principle, the chief executive and
judge, *pontifex maximus* and supreme commander. A not uncommon epithet
of ancient Near Eastern kings was "the good shepherd", [7] a title which is
often found in Assyrian building inscriptions. In addition, the king was
frequently called *iššiak Aššur*, Assur's vicar, [8] a phrase expressing the basic
ideology of the king's position; he ruled over the country of the god. [9] Other

---

[5] Ira M. Price, "Some Observations on the Financial Importance of the temple in
the 1'st Dynasty of Babylon", *AJSL* 32, 1915–16, pp. 250 ff., A. Deimel, *Sumerische
Tempelwirtschaft* (Analecta Orientalia 2), 1931, A. Goetze, *Hethiter, Churriter und
Assyrer* (Instittutet for sammenlignende Kulturforskning. Serie A:XVII), Oslo 1936,
p. 10, A.L. Oppenheim, "The Mesopotamian Temple", *BA* 7/44, pp. 54 ff., I.J. Gelb,
"The Arua Institution", *RA* 66/72, pp. 10 ff., Kilian Butz, "Konzentrationen wirt-
schaftlicher Macht im Königreich Larsa: Der Nanna-Ningal Tempelkomplex in Ur",
Wiener Zeitschrift für die Kunde des Morgenlandes 65/66, 1973–74, pp. 1 ff., A.
Falkenstein, "La cité-temple sumérienne", *CHM* 1, 1954, pp. 784 ff. (Engl. ed., *The
Sumerian Temple City*, transl. by Maria de J. Ellis, [Sources and Monographs; Monographs in History. Ancient Near East 1/1], Los Angeles 1974). Cf. also H.G. Güterbock, "The Hittite Temple According to Written Sources", *Le Temple et le Culte* (RAI
20) Leiden, 1975, pp. 128 f.

[6] It has been maintained that from a religious point of view building temples can
be seen as increasing and securing the holiness of the nation, J. Pedersen, *Israel* III-IV,
p. 238, Aa. Bentzen, "The Cultic Use of the Story of the Ark in Samuel", *JBL* 67/48,
pp. 47 f., A.S. Kapelrud, "Temple Building, a Task for Gods and Kings", *Orientalia*
32/36, pp. 56ff.

[7] A Badaway, *op. cit.*, p. 108, A. Falkenstein, *The Sumerian Temple City*, p. 19.
Cf. J.A. Wilson, "The Function of the State", in *Before Philosophy*, by H. & H.A.
Frankfort, J.A. Wilson and T. Jacobsen, Chicago (1946), 1972, pp. 88 f.

[8] M. Trolle Larsen, "The City and its King. On the Old Assyrian Notion of Kingship", *Le palais et la royauté* (RAI XIX, Paris 1971), Paris 1974, p. 288. For references,
see M.J. Seux, *Épithètes royales akkadiennes et sumériennes*, Paris 1967, pp. 110 ff.
Even if it was rare a New kingdom Pharaoh could be called "deputy regent" (* idnw*) of
his god, see Virginia Condon, *Seven Royal Hymns of the Ramesside Period. Papyrus
Turin CG54031* (Münchener Ägyptologische Studien 37), München 1978, plate 87:2.
For *idn*, "govern as a deputy", see A. Gardiner, "The Coronation of King Haremhab",
JEA 39, 1953, p. 18, note v., cf. J. Murnane, *Ancient Egyptian Coregencies* (SAOC
40), Chicago 1977, p. 59.

[9] For example, according to S.N. Kramer, the ruler of Lagash was the representative of the god who was the real ruler of the city of Lagash, "Sumerian Historiography",
IEJ 3/53, p. 227. Similarly, the Israelite king can be seen as the vice regent of his god,

descriptive epithets for the king were *aklu(m)*, "overseer"[10] and the priest title *šangû*, "administrator". The king administered the god's territory and his people.[11] Consequently, the people of the nation were the subjects of the god[12] and lived in his *ba'ūlatum*, "dominion."[13]

The cosmological aspect of the city has its roots in the idea of the city as the abode of the god,[14] the ruler of cosmos and nation. Because the temple, as the visible expression of his domain,[15] was, at the same time, the king's property, the capital was the ruling center of both the god and his vice regent (Akkad. *šakkanakku*),[16] the king.[17] Therefore, temple and palace should be

Yahweh. Moreover, the title משיח, "the annointed one", may designate the king's special relationship to Yahweh. Through the annointment ritual he is commissioned to govern Yahweh's people, cf. A.R. Johnson, "Hebrew Conceptions of Kingship", *Myth, Ritual, and Kingship*, ed. S.H. Hooke, Oxford 1958, pp. 207 f. R. de Vaux interprets this relationship as the king having become a vassal of Yahweh, "Le roi d'Israël, vassal de Yahwé", *Mélanges E. Tisserant*, I (Studi e Testi 231), Rome 1964, pp. 119 ff. (Engl. transl. in *The Bible and the Ancient Near East*, Garden City, N.Y., 1971, pp. 152 ff.). For T. Mettinger, this is a contractual relationship, *King and Messiah* (Coniectanea Biblica. Old Testament Series 8), Lund 1976, pp. 208 ff. For the Psalmist it is one of sonship to Yahweh, Ps. 2:7.

[10] E. Weidner, "Hof- und Harems-Erlasse assyrischer Könige aus dem 2. Jahrtausend v. Chr.", *AfO* 17/54-56, p. 269.

[11] P. Garelli, "Les temples et le pouvoir royal en Assyrie du XIVe au VIIIe siècle", *Le Temple et le Culte* (RAI 20), Leiden 1975, pp. 116 ff. For *šangû* see Nikolaus Schneider, "Der šangû als Verwaltungsbehörde und Opfergabenspender im Reiche der dritten Dynastie von Ur", *JCS* 1/47, pp. 122 ff., and W. von Soden, *Akkadisches Handwörterbuch*, Lieferung 13, 1976, *s.v.*

[12] Cf., for instance, D.D. Luckenbill, *The Annals of Sennacherib* (OIP II), Chicago 1924, p. 103, line 37. One should note that because the king is the "representative of the divine ruler, rebellion is not simply described as an act of disobedience towards a human master but is regarded as insubordination against the god himself," B. Albrektson, *History and the Gods. An Essay on the Idea of Historical Events as Divine Manifestations in the Ancient Near East and in Israel* (Coniectanea Biblica. OT Series 1), Lund 1967, p. 49.

[13] I.J. Gelb, *Glossary of Old Akkadian* (Materials for the Assyrian Dictionary 3), Chicago 1957, p. 90.

[14] For the city "endowed with divine attributes" and identified with the god, see, for example, R. Yaron, *The Laws of Eshnunna*, Jerusalem 1969, p. 73.

[15] For the temple ideology, see, for instance, G.W. Ahlström, "Heaven on Earth — at Hazor and Arad", *Religious Syncretism in Antiquity*, ed. by B.A. Pearson, Missoula, Mont. 1975, pp. 67 ff. For the temple as the god's estate, see E. Sollberger, "The Temple in Babylonia" in *Le Temple et le Culte* (RAI 20), Leiden 1975, pp. 31 ff.

[16] For *šakkanakku* see, for example, W.W. Hallo, *Early Mesopotamian Royal Titles: A Philological and Historical Analysis* (American Oriental Series 43), New Haven 1957, pp. 100 ff., cf. J.-R. Kupper, "Rois et šakkanakku", *JCS* 21/67, pp. 123 ff., and B. Albrektson, *History and the Gods*, pp. 45 ff. M.-J. Seux, *Épithètes royales akkadiennes et sumériennes*, pp. 276 ff.

[17] Cf. Eric Uphill, "The Concept of the Egyptian Palace as a 'Ruling Machine'," *Man, Settlement and Urbanism*, ed. by Peter J. Ucko, Ruth Tringham and G.W. Dimbley, Cambridge, Mass., 1972, pp. 721 ff.

seen as two aspects of the same phenomenon; together they constituted the essence of the state.[18]

What has been said above helps to explain why a walled acropolis[19] was usually built to separate the divine and royal palaces from the rest of the city. Gods and kings were no ordinary beings. The acropolis should be construed as the center of the universe,[20] a concept reflected in the architectural plan of ancient Ebla (Tell Mardikh in Syria). It depicts an acropolis center composed of a palace and temple complex and a lower city built in four quarters, each of which could be entered through gates in the city wall.[21] It is possible that this city plan was inspired by a similar Sumerian layout.[22]

The city plan of Hittite Carchemish shows a citadel mound with temples in the northeast, an inner walled town and an outer walled city.[23] At Hazor,

---

[18] With this understanding of the temple it should be quite clear that the "destruction of a Sumerian temple was the most disastrous calamity that could befall a city and its people", S.N. Kramer, *The Sumerians. Their History, Culture, and Character*, Chicago 1963, p. 142. The destruction of the Jerusalem temple and the Judean nation is another example of the nation, the god's territory, being eradicated. It was, therefore, mandatory to build a new temple when people returned from the Babylonian Exile. The god's domain had to be rebuilt.

[19] For the term "acropolis" in its Greek setting, see Astrid Wokalek, *Griechische Stadtbefestigungen. Studien zur Geschichte der frühgriechischen Befestigungsanlagen* (Abhandlungen zur Kunst-, Musik- und Literaturwissenschaft 136), Bonn 1973, pp. 13–24.

[20] See M. Liverani, "Memorandum on the Approach to Historiographic Texts", *Orientalia* 42/73, pp. 189 ff. See also B. Alster who refers to the well-known fact that one thought of both city and temple as having their prototypes in heaven, "Early Patterns in Mesopotamian Literature", *Kramer Anniversary Volume* (AOAT 17), 1976, p. 19.

[21] G. Pettinato and P. Matthiae, "Aspetti amministrativi e topografici di Ebla nel III meillennio Av. Cr.", *Rivista degli Studi Orientali* 50/76, pp. 1 ff., and p. 28, fig. Cf. G. Pettinato, "The Royal Archives of Tell Mardikh-Ebla", *BA* 39/76, p. 47, P. Matthiae, "Ebla in the Late Early Syrian Period: The Royal Palace and the State Archives", *BA* 39/76, p. 99. For the excavations, see now P. Matthiae, *Ebla. An Empire Rediscovered*, Garden City, N.Y., 1981. For the reading Ibla, see I.J. Gelb, "Thoughts about Ibla: A Preliminary Evaluation, March 1977", *Syro-Mesopotamian Studies* 1/77, pp. 3-30.

[22] Cf. M. Hammond, assisted by L.J. Barton, *The City in the Ancient World*, Cambridge, Mass., 1972, pp. 37 f. For the planning of cities, see Paul Lampl, *Cities and Planning in the Ancient Near East*, New York 1968, and H. Frankfort, "Town Planning in Ancient Mesopotamia", *The Town Planning Review* 21/50, pp. 98 ff. J.A. Gallary, "Town Planning and Community Structure", *The Legacy of Sumer*, ed. by Denise Schmandt-Besserat (Bibliotheca Mesopotamica IV), Malibu 1976, pp. 69 ff.

[23] L. Woolley–R.D. Barnett, *Carchemish III. The excavations in the inner Town and the Hittite Inscriptions*, London 1952, cf. H. Güterbock, "The Deeds of Suppiluliuma as told by his son, Mursili II", *JCS* 10/56, p. 95, AIII: 33, *id.*, "The Hittite Temple", *Le Temple et le Culte* (RAI 20), Leiden 1975, p. 125. Cf. also K.M. Kenyon, *Amorites and Canaanites*, pp. 70 f., K.-H. Bernhardt, *Die Umwelt des Alten Testaments*, 2d ed. Berlin 1968, pp. 190 f.

the MB-LB acropolis was in the south with an (assumed) palace and temple precinct (Area A).[24] Israel's last capital, Samaria, should also be mentioned although we do not know of any temple on its acropolis due to the incomplete excavations there. Another site to be considered is Jerusalem. When Solomon built his palace and temple complex, he followed the Syro-Palestinian pattern of separating the royal buildings from the rest of the city.[25] The geography also invited such a separation.

That the acropolis phenomenon was very common in Syria – Palestine is evident from the fact that nearly half of all Early Bronze Age III sites in southwestern Palestine had an acropolis surrounded by a wall. The rest of the city was constructed on a lower level.[26] As other examples from the Levant one can mention Zincirli (Sam'al) which had an acropolis built on a hill in the center of the city,[27] Qatna, Alalakh, Alişar,[28] Kamid el-Loz, Tell ed-Duweir[29] and probably also Mesha's capital, Dibon.[30]

As mentioned above, the capital was the ruling center of the nation (the territory of the god). More specifically, the acropolis was this center and, as such, provided the basis for the king's functions and policies. Narrowing it down even farther, it may be said with A. Falkenstein that the temple was the "nucleus of the state."[31] Ideologically, the main god of the nation or

[24] Y. Yadin, *Hazor. The Head of all those Kingdoms, Joshua 11:10* (The Schweich Lectures of the British Academy 1970), London 1972, p. 103.

[25] Cf. Th. Busink, *Der Tempel von Jerusalem* I, p. 153 ff., and fig. 47. It is possible that the Zion fortress, מצדת ציון, which David's men took via the *şinnor* (water shaft?) was the Jebusite acropolis of Jerusalem, 2 Sam. 5:7, 9. For the *şinnor*, cf. K.M. Kenyon, *Digging up Jerusalem,* New York and Washington 1974, pp. 84 ff. For the ease with which David took Jerusalem, see Ahlström, "Was David a Jebusite Subject?", *ZAW* 92/80, pp. 285 ff.

[26] Valerie M. Fargo, *Settlement in Southern Palestine during Early Bronze III,* (Unpubl. diss. Univ. of Chicago), Chicago 1979, pp. 88 f.

[27] Cf. H. Klengel, *Geschichte und Kultur Altsyriens,* Heidelberg 1967, pp. 144 f.

[28] R. Naumann, *Architektur Kleinasiens,* 1955, pp. 363 ff., *et passim,* and fig. 445. Cf. Th.A. Busink, *Der Tempel von Jerusalem* I, Leiden 1970, pp. 538 ff.

[29] O. Tufnell *et al., Lachish III. The Iron Age,* London 1953, pp. 78 ff.

[30] For Dibon's *qrhh,* see below. Röllig compares Mesha's acropolis buildings with those of Solomon, *KAI* II, p. 171. In Transjordan an EB-MB city with an acropolis has been found at Jawa, see S.W. Helms, "Jawa Excavations 1974. A Preliminary Report", *Levant* 8/76, pp. 1 ff. At Buşeirah (biblical Bozra?) in southern Jordan an "acropolis" protected by "a massive fortification wall" has been found. It dates probably from the 8th century B.C. The buildings inside the wall have been labelled "palace or temple structure". The style of both of the buildings and the fortifications is different from what is known from Edom at this time. The explanation given is that the style could "reflect Assyrian influences" and, thus, the buildings would be from a time when Edom was a vassal to Assyria, Chrystal-M. Bennett, "Excavations at Buseirah, Southern Jordan 1972: Preliminary Report", *Levant* 6/74, pp. 1 ff.

[31] *The Sumerian Temple City,* p. 7.

city-state was the 'father' of the king[32] who reigned on his behalf,[33] cf. Pss. 2:7; 89:27. This intimate relationship between god and king is expressed, for example, in the Sumerian epic of "Enmerkar and the Lord of Aratta."[34] Both were said to live in the same building complex and, moreover, seem to have shared the same throneroom.[35] The inference is, therefore, that the royal throne was divine.[36]

The King as the administrator of the God's territory

The above makes quite understandable the fact that religion and religious policy were part of the king's duties. Indeed, it is evident that the king, as the administrator of his god's territory, was not only the organizer and the builder of the country[37] but was, in principle, the organizer of the cult as well. A few examples should be cited. A Hittite text states that the storm god made the king, the *labarna*, the governor of the land of Hatti.[38] In Egypt the "supreme god, Rē, entrusted the land to his son, the king."[39] In the

---

[32] Å.W. Sjöberg, "Die göttliche Abstammung der sumerisch-babylonischen Herrscher", *Orientalia Suecana* 21/72, pp. 87-112. Cf. also I. Engnell, *Studies in Divine Kingship in the Ancient Near East*, Uppsala 1943, p. 16, G.W. Ahlström, "Solomon, the Chosen One", *History of Religions* 8/68, p. 94, M. Weinfeld, *Deuteronomy and the Deuteronomic School*, Oxford 1972, p. 80.

[33] The king can be seen as the personification of the state, cf. J.A. Wilson, *Before Philosophy*, p. 98. Concerning the Israelite kingship it must be seen from the same viewpoints. It would be impossible to maintain – as does the tendentious writer of 1 Sam. 8:7 – that the "inauguration" of the kingship meant that the king usurped Yahweh's position. A nation without a king was, properly speaking, an unthinkable entity.

[34] S.N. Kramer, *Enmerkar and the Lord of Aratta*, Philadelphia 1952, p. 38, lines 534 ff.

[35] Cf. A. Falkenstein, *op. cit.*, p. 12.

[36] This is the ideological background for Ps. 45:7, and also for Solomon having been chosen to sit on Yahweh's throne, I Chr. 28:5, 29:23, 2 Chr. 9:8. According to F. Canciani and G. Pettinato, king Solomon's throne was (in some way) patterned after the types known from Ugarit and Phoenicia which had their prototypes in Egypt, "Salomos Throne, Philologische und archäologische Erwägungen," *ZDPV* 81/65, pp. 88 ff. Compare also R.J. Williams, "A People Come out of Egypt", *SVT* 28, 1974, p. 243.

[37] "Responsibility for foreign as for domestic policy rested ultimately with the god who, as owner and ruler of the state, made his commands known to the king, his earthly delegate, by means of omens." J.M. Munn-Rankin, "Diplomacy in Western Asia in the Early Second Millennium B.C.", *Iraq* 18/56, p. 70.

[38] For the text see A. Goetze (in a review of H. Bozkurt, M. Çığ, H.G. Güterbock, *Istanbul Arkeoloji Müzelerinde Bulunan Bogazköy Tableterinden Seçme Metinler*, 1944), *JCS* 1/47, pp. 90 f.

[39] J.A. Wilson, "The Function of the State", in *Before Philosophy*, by H. and H.A. Frankfort, J.A. Wilson, and T. Jacobsen, Chicago (1946), 1972, p. 81.

prologue to his law code, Hammurapi of Babylon emphasizes that it is he who is the

za-ni-nu-um na-'-du-um ša É.KUR	devoted caretaker of Ekur
LUGAL *le-iu-um mu-te-er* ^{uru}NUN^{ki}	the mighty king, restorer of Eridu
a-na aš-ri-šu mu-ub-bi-ib	on its place, the one who has purified
šu-luḫ É.ZU.AB	the rituals[40] of Eabzu

Codex Ham. I : 60ff.

Further, Hammurapi says that he is the one who

mu-šar-bu-ú šar-ru-ti-šu	enlarged his kingdom
da-rí-íš i-ši-mu	(who) forever prescribed
zi-bi el-lu-tim	pure sacrifices.

Codex Ham. IV : 19ff.

Here the king describes himself as caretaker, restorer and organizer of the temples and their cults.[41] In principle, the king enables the divine right and justice to be established in his kingdom.

The Mari documents also illustrate how royal government regulated religious practice. For example, not only could the king sacrifice but he could decide dates for festivals and sacrifices in the provinces.[42] Moreover, he had a number of gods transported to the capital so that they could receive official service.[43]

From Mesopotamia a few other examples may be cited. In an inscription Tiglath-Pileser I relates that Aššur and the great gods commissioned him to enlarge their country, Assyria.[44] It should be noted that the king used the ex-

---

[40] This may mean that Hammurapi regulated the cult. For the king as *zānin ēkalli*, "sustainer of the temple" (or, caretaker), cf. I. Engnell, *Studies in Divine Kingship in the Ancient Near East*, Uppsala 1943, pp. 31, 155.

[41] See, for instance, also Nabunaid's inscription about his rise to power (*VAB* 4, No. 8, p. 277, cf. *ANET*, pp. 308 f.) where he mentions Neriglissar's restoration of Babylonian sanctuaries which had been destroyed by the Manda people. Cf. also the Cylinder of Neriglissar, *VAB* 4, No. 1, pp. 209 ff. (text CT XXXVI: 7).

[42] M. Birot, *Lettres de Yaqqim-Addu, gouverneur de Sagarâtum* (ARM XIV), Paris 1974, texts 8 and 9. Cf. A.L. Oppenheim, "The Archives of the Palace of Mari, II", *JNES* 13/54, p. 142, A. Finet, "La place du devin dans la société de Mari", *RAI* 14, Paris 1966, p. 92. See also B.F. Butto, *Studies on Women at Mari*, Baltimore 1974, pp. 17 ff.

[43] G. Dossin, "Le panthéon de Mari", *Studia Mariana*, ed. by A. Parrot, Leiden 1950, pp. 44 f., cf. V.H. Matthews, "Government Involvement in the Religion of the Mari Kingdom", *RA* 72/78, pp. 151 ff.

[44] See P. Garelli, "Le temples et le pouvoir royal en Assyrie du XIVe au VIIIe siècle", *Le Temple et le Culte* (RAI 20), Leiden 1975, p. 117, cf. A.K. Grayson, *Assyrian Royal Inscriptions* 2, Wiesbaden 1976, p. 6.

pression 'their country' which is in agreement with the political and religious ideology. Another inscription states that Marduk entrusted Nabu-apla-iddina with organization of the cult, its rites and sacrifices.[45] When Sennacherib occupied Hirimmu during his first campaign, he not only reorganized it as an Assyrian province but stipulated that the "choicest" sacrifices should be offered "for the gods of Aššur, my lords... forever."[46] Esarhaddon did the same after conquering Egypt in 671 B.C.[47] In another text Sennacherib says that the god Aššur will name a descendant of Sennacherib "for the shepherd-ship of the land and people" and that this future king will undertake some building activities.[48] Here we should observe that building projects are connected with the idea of the king as the shepherd of his god's people.[49]

From what has been said above, it should be evident that religion was an arm of the royal administration. By sending out and placing military personnel and civil servants including priests in district capitals, at strategic points, in store cities, and in the national sanctuaries, the central government saw to it that both civil and cultic laws were upheld and that taxes were paid. This was extremely important when a conquered area was added to the nation or when a new city was built.[50] Especially instructive is an example from the time of Sargon II. After building Dūr-Sharrukīn and settling foreigners in the new city, Sargon also installed Assyrian officials such as overseers (aklū)[51] to teach the people the ways of Assyria, "to revere (fear, respect) god and king" (palāḫ ili u šarri).[52] Because life was steered by the gods, religion was at the base of all human and national existence. Consequently, the Sargon quotation cannot be limited to refer to taxes for "royal and temple needs" only, as M. Cogan suggests.[53] Here the phrase palāḫ ili refers to the national religion.

These examples show that the Mesopotamian king was, in principle, the organizer of the cult, the foundation of the nation's life. As will be shown

---

[45] L.W. King, *Babylonian Boundary-Stones and Memorial-Tablets in the British Museum,* London 1912, pp. 122 f., col. II: 29 ff. – III: 10. See also W.G. Lambert (rev. of F. Gössmann, "Das Era Epos"), *AfO* 18/57-58, p. 398.

[46] D.D. Luckenbill, *The Annals of Sennacherib* (Oriental Institute Publications II), Chicago 1924, p. 57, lines 18-19, cf. p. 55, lines 58-59, and p. 67, lines 8-9.

[47] R. Borger, *Die Inschriften Asarhaddons, Königs von Assyrien,* Graz 1956, pp. 45 f., H.W.F. Saggs, *The Greatness that was Babylon,* New York 1962, p. 242.

[48] A.K. Grayson, "The Walters Art Gallery Sennacherib Inscription", *AfO* 20/64, p. 96.

[49] Cf. Nebukadressar's "Bauinschrift", S. Langdon, *VAB* 4, No. 11, 1912, p. 99.

[50] Cf. A.L. Oppenheim, *Ancient Mesopotamia,* p. 119.

[51] It would, perhaps, be possible to see some government officials as having both religious and non-religious duties, as was the case in Egypt, see below, p. 15.

[52] *CAD* I A: 1, *s.v.,* p. 278.

[53] *Imperialism and Religion: Assyria, Judah and Israel in the Eighth and Seventh Centuries B.C.E.,* Missoula, Mont., 1974, p. 51.

below, the same principle can be found in other parts of the ancient Near East [54] where religion was part of the national government's activities. The cultic calendar provided the framework within which life for both nation and nature was maintained and regulated. Indeed, the cult established the right contact between god and nation and through its festivals, the divine order was established and the will of the gods was made known.

---

[54] A parallel ideology exists in Southeast Asia. Here kingship is understood as "the wielder of dharma and the organizer of this world in its aspects as polity and as a link between the cosmological levels of heavens of gods and the level of this world of humans." S.J. Tambiah, *World Conquerer and World Renouncer* (Chapter 7: "The Galactic Polity"), Cambridge Studies in Antropology 15, Cambridge 1976, p. 108. Thus, one can find that "the king, his palace, his capital are the pivots and embodiments of the kingdom... the divine mountain was not only physically reproduced in the capital, but was identified with the palace itself," *op. cit.,* p. 115.

CHAPTER TWO

BUILDING OF CITIES AND FORTRESSES AS A POLITICAL TOOL

In the preceding chapter the phenomenon of urbanization was described as an ongoing political process. Further examples of this type of activity and other royal building projects will be discussed in what follows. For instance, "The Instructions for Merikarê" (21st century B.C.) are illustrative in this regard.[1] Merikarê was "told" by the Pharaoh, his father, to construct large fortified cities and fortresses in the eastern Delta. The rationale behind the order was to protect the area from plundering by enemies (the ' ꜣmw) who, according to the text, usually attacked the small, unprotected settlements, while avoiding the larger fortified cities.[2]

During the 12th dynasty when Egypt occupied Nubia, the Pharaohs built fortresses and towns not only to stabilize conquered areas,[3] but to bind them securely to the Egyptian administration and to protect trade.[4] From an architectural point of view, the fortifications around these towns "appear to be unmodified copies of a type of temple enclosure wall in Egypt itself.[5]

---

[1] A. Volten, *Zwei altägyptische politische Schriften. Die Lehre für König Merikarê (Pap. Carlsberg VI) und die Lehre des Königs Amenemhet*, København 1945, pp. 50ff., cf. R.O. Faulkner in *The Literature of Ancient Egypt*, ed. by W.K. Simpson, New Haven and London 1977, pp. 180 ff., J.A. Wilson, *ANET*, pp. 414 ff.

[2] This text was understood as a propoganda tract by Merikarê himself, see E. Otto, *Ägypten. Der Weg der Pharaonenreiches*, Stuttgart 1953 (1958), p. 101, A. Scharff, "Der historische Abschnitt der Lehre für König Merikarê," *Sitzungsberichte der Bayerischen Akademie der Wissenschaften* 8, 1936, pp. 6 f., A. Volten, *op. cit.*, pp. 53 ff., T. Säve-Söderbergh, *Pharaohs and Mortals* (transl. by R.E. Oldenburg), Indianapolis and New York 1961, p. 65, A. Badaway, "The Civic Sense of Pharaoh and Urban Development in Ancient Egypt," *Journal of the American Research Center in Egypt* 6/67, p. 105, W. Helck, *Die Beziehungen Ägyptens zu Vorderasien im 3. und 2. Jahrtausend v. Chr.*, Wiesbaden 1971, p. 39. See also Th.L. Thompson, *The Historicity of the Patriarchal Narratives* (BZAW 133), Berlin 1974, pp. 139ff.

[3] T. Säve-Söderbergh, *Ägypten und Nubien. Ein Beitrag zur Geschichte altägyptischer Aussenpolitik*, Lund 1941, pp. 80 ff., cf. also W.A. Ward, "Egypt and the East Mediterranean in the Early Second Millennium B.C.," *Orientalia* 30/61, p. 143, K.-H. Bernhardt, "Verwaltungspraxis im spätbronzezeitlichen Palästina," *Beiträge zur sozialen Sturktur des alten Vorderasien* (Schriften zur Geschichte und Kultur des Alten Orient), ed. by Horst Klengel, Berlin 1971, p. 135.

[4] S. Clarke, "Ancient Egyptian Frontier Fortresses," *JEA* 3/16, pp. 155ff., cf. A.H. Gardiner, "An Ancient Egyptian List of the Fortresses of Nubia," *JEA* 3/16, pp. 184ff.

[5] B.J. Kemp, "Fortified Towns in Nubia," *Man, Settlement and Urbanism*, ed. by Peter J. Ucko, Ruth Tringham and G.W. Dimbleby, Cambridge, Mass., 1972, p. 653.

Further, the Pharaohs of the New Kingdom built temples in Nubia in order to "teach" the people of the area the Egyptian way of life.[6] Ramses II built a fortress temple at Zaweit Umm el-Rakham, 25 km west of Mersa Matruh,[7] and constructed others along the Mediterranean protecting the border with Libya.[8] Behind the phenomenon of establishing temple forts is the idea that they symbolize the power of the country, namely, god and king.[9] Consequently, both military and cultic personnel should be well represented throughout the god's (and king's) territory.

Although Egypt dominated Palestine during the period of the New Kingdom, an exact parallel with the situation in Nubia cannot be drawn. Palestine was neither incorporated as a province of the Egyptian empire nor was it occupied by the military. Thus, from an administrative point of view, Palestine's status was different from that of Nubia. Indeed, in order to show that its legal status was not that of a provine, it is best termed an Egyptian "dominion".[10] Its kings or petty princes were the Pharaoh's vassals who, together with an Egyptian official (a native or an Egyptian), were responsible for keeping the area under the rule of the Egyptian king. Scattered Egyptian military bases did exist in Palestine and the administrative center was at Gaza where there was an Amun temple.[11] The Harris papyrus mentions nine towns in Canaan that belonged to the estate of Amun.[12] In addition, Egypt-

---

[6] Cf. H. Kees, "Ägypten," *Kulturgeschichte des Alten Orients I* (Handbuch der Altertumswissenschaft III, 1.3.I), München 1933, pp. 349f., T. Säve-Söderberg, *Ägypten und Nubien*, pp. 189ff., 200ff. The temples at Abu Simbel and at Soleb are from this time.

[7] L. Habachi, "Découverte d'un temple-fortress de Ramsès II," in "Les grandes découvertes archéologiques de 1954," *La Revue du Caire* 33, 1955, pp. 62ff.

[8] Cf. K.A. Kitchen, *The Third Intermediate Period in Egypt (1100–650 B.C.)*, Warminster 1973, p. 244.

[9] According to W.C. Hayes, the temples functioned as departments of "the royal administration," "Egypt: Internal Affairs from Thutmosis I to the death of Amenophis III," *CAH* II:1, p. 328, cf. p. 359.

[10] D.G. Hogarth distinguished three degrees of suzerainity in the Egyptian dominated areas. The first is "territorial dominion secured by permanent occupation." The second degree "meant permanent tributary allegiance" and did not include occupation of the country. Because of the fear of reconquest, only "a few garrisons and agents and the prestige of the conquerer" were needed. The third degree was "little more than a sphere of exclusive influence, from which tribute was expected." Hogarth places Palestine in the second group, "Egyptian Empire in Asia," *JEA* 1/14, pp. 9f.

[11] The Papyrus Harris 9, 1-2, cf. W. Helck, *Die Beziehungen Ägyptens*, pp. 444f. The LB Hathor temple at Timna may also be mentioned, see B. Rothenberg, *Were These King Solomon's Mines?*, New York, 1972, pp. 125ff., 201. However, this area and the whole of Sinai, may have been part of Egypt during this time. Even if the temple is characterized as Egyptian, from an archaeological point of view, it had a local layout.

[12] Cf. W. Helck, *op. cit.*, p. 252, J.A. Wilson in *ANET*, pp. 260f.

ian inspired temples have been found at Beth-Shan[13] and Jaffa.[14] In most other places the Pharaohs erected stelae showing themselves worshipping Canaanite gods, a phenomenon which *could* point to an identification of Egyptian gods with the Canaanite deities.[15] In a vassal country the indigenous gods had to be worshipped because they "governed" the life of both men and nature. The existence of the Amun temple at Gaza may be seen as an indication of the area's status as a dominion. Amun was the overlord allowing the other gods to do their usual and necessary work.

In the Hittite empire, several of the temples were centers of the "civil government"[16] and of the economy. As such, they "must have housed a very large staff of religious and civil functionaries,"[17] all of whom were government appointees. A Hittite text containing instructions for commanders in border areas evinces the royal concern for the cult and the maintenance of the temples in these areas. The commanders of the border guards had to inspect the temples and insure not only that the cult of the country was performed, but that the temples were kept in good condition. If necessary, the commander had to make sure that the temples were restored or rebuilt.[18]

In Syria we know that the Hittites built a line of "square-walled fortress-towns from Qadesh (Tell Nebi Mend) on the Orontes to Jusuf Pacha on the Euphrates, with Qatna (ca. 100 ha.) as its best known stronghold."[19] This line of fortified towns was not intended solely as protection against Egypt. Its purpose was to secure the empire against invading tribes and to keep the population of the area under Hittite political and religious control. Therefore, the sanctuaries of these fortress-towns may be seen as part of the royal government.

---

[13] A. Rowe, *The Four Canaanite Temples of Beth Shan,* II:1, Philadelphia, p. 1049, cf. the discussion in H.O. Thompson, *Mekal, The God of Beth-Shan,* Leiden 1970, pp. 16ff, and W. Helck, *op. cit.,* p. 444.

[14] H. and J. Kaplan, "Jaffa," *Encyclopedia of Archaeological Excavations in the Holy Land,* III, Jerusalem 1976, p. 540.

[15] Concerning these problems, see also A. Alt, "Ägyptische Tempel in Palästina und die Landnahme der Philister," *ZDPV* 67/44, pp. 1ff. (= *KS* I, 1953, pp. 216ff.). One exception that should be mentioned is Byblos. This city considered itself almost Egyptian. Thus, the Baalat (Ashtarte) of Byblos was identified with the Egyptian goddess Hathor, cf. R. Stadelmann, *Syrisch-palästinensische Gottheiten in Ägypten* (Probleme der Ägyptologie 15), Leiden 1967, p. 98.

[16] For the king as temple builder, see F. Starke, "Ḫalmašuit im Anitta-Text und die hethitische Ideologie von Königtum," *ZfA* 69/79, pp. 59f.

[17] O.R. Gurney, *The Hittites,* London 1952, p. 145.

[18] See A. Goetze, "From the Instructions for the Commander of the Border Guards," *ANET,* 1950, pp. 210f., cf. H.G. Güterbock, "The Hittite Temple According to Written Sources," *Le Temple et le Culte* (RAI 20), Leiden 1975, p. 128.

[19] W.J. van Liere, "Capitals and Citadels of Bronze-Iron Age Syria in their Relationship to Land and Water," *Annales archéologiques de Syrie* 13/63, pp. 109ff.

Several other examples from the Levant of kings as city builders should be mentioned. On a Hadad statue from Zincirli (8th century B.C.), king Panammu I stated that he was given a command by the gods (probably through a prophet) to build and restore a number of cities.[20] King Zakkur of Hamath and Luash (8th century B.C.) reports in an inscription[21] that, after having built Ḥazrak, he built strongholds and temples throughout his kingdom. In addition, the text mentions that Zakkur built, or rebuilt, Afis (*'āpēš*) and "[let the gods live in] the temple [of Iluwer]."[22] According to a Luwian-Phoenician bilingual inscription from Karatepe (8th century B.C.), Azitawadda built fortresses and cities in the conquered areas and ordered people to settle in them.[23] In one of the cities he built, Azitawaddiya, he installed (ישב) a god, Baal-KRNTRYŠ, and sacrificed to all the gods.[24] Settling people in a conquered area implies that the king ordered some of his own subjects to move to the territory. Their function was to promote stability and control. Building temples and "installing gods"[25] in the area fulfilled the same function. Such temples were part of the royal administration and, thus, were state property since the realm of the king and the realm of the god were one and the same.

The so-called Moabite stone (9th century B.C.) offers information not only about king Mesha's initiative in building and rebuilding cities, but also

---

[20] Donner-Röllig, *KAI* text 214:10. J.C.L. Gibson understands זררי, קרית, and כפירי as cities, towns and villages, *Textbook of Syrian Semitic Inscriptions* II, Oxford 1975, pp. 66ff.

[21] *KAI*, text 202.

[22] For a reconstruction of the text, see Gibson, *op. cit.*, text 5B: 4-13. For the reading Zakkur, see J.C. Greenfield, "The Dialects of Early Aramaic," *JNES* 37/78, p. 93, n. 9, cf. T. Nöldecke, "Aramäische Inschriften," *ZfA* 21/08, p. 376, M. Lidzbarski, *Ephemeris für semitische Epigraphik,* Giessen 1915, pp. 3ff., A.R. Millard, "Epigraphic Notes, Aramaic and Hebrew," *PEQ* 110/78, p. 23. M. Black has drawn attention to the parallel with Mesha of Moab, "The Zakir Stele," in *Documents from Old Testament Times,* ed. D. Winton Thomas, London 1958, p. 250.

[23] *KAI*, text 26:I:13ff., cf. M. Miller, "The Moabite Stone as a Memorial Stela," *PEQ* 106/74, p. 14.

[24] Col. II:17ff. In Col. III:18f. the text has *b'l šmm el qn 'rṣ wšmš 'lm wkl dr bn 'lm* ("Baal of the Heavens, El the "owner/ruler" of the earth [see my *Aspects of Syncretism,* pp. 74f.], and Šamaš of eternity and the whole assembly of gods"). The Luwian version has rendered Baal ŠMM with *tipasas* Tarḫunzas, i.e. Tarḫunzas of the Heavens, El *qn 'rṣ* with the sun of heaven, and Šamaš *'lm* with Ea. This may show that the Luwian scribes were not too familiar with the Semitic deities and their names. For instance, every time they saw the name Baal they translated it with Tarḫunzas, H.G. Güterbock (oral communication). For a discussion of these deity names, see also M. Weippert, "Element phönikischer und kilikischer Religion in den Inschriften vom Karatepe," *XVII. Deutscher Orientalistentag vom 21. bis 27. Juli 1968 in Würzburg, Vorträge,* I (ZDMG Suppl. I:1), Wiesbaden 1969, pp. 191–217. For the Luwian text, see J.D. Hawkins and A. Mopurgo Davies, "On the Problems of Karatepe: The Hieroglyphic Text," *Anatolian Studies* 28/78, pp. 103-119.

[25] *KAI* II, p. 41.

about an Israelite king's activity in the same sphere. Mesha mentions (ll. 9ff.) that the Israelite king (Omri or Ahab) built both 'Aṭarot and Jahaṣ. In the war of liberation against the Israelites, Mesha captured these two cities among others. As a רית (gift?)[26] to Chemosh and Moab, he killed all the people of 'Aṭarot and brought the אראל of its god Dod[27] to his god Chemosh (ll. 12f.). The same treatment was accorded to another captured city, namely, Nebo (ll. 14–18). The כלי or לי[רא]א of its god Yahweh were dragged before Chemosh. It is possible that both the כלי and the אראלי are either symbols of these two Israelite deities or holy vessels. As such they were brought as trophies to Chemosh, the main god of the Moabites, who was also honored with the slaughter of the population of these two cities. The gods of the Israelites were thus nullified, the people annihilated, and 'Aṭarot was repopulated with Mesha's own people.[28]

Subsequently, Mesha annexed Jahaṣ to Dibon (l. 20).[29] Although we are not told whether there was a sanctuary in Jahaṣ, it is probable that this town, like other cities, had its own cult place. This assumption is supported by Josh. 21:36 (codices L, C and Ben Hayim) and I Chr. 6:78, which mention that Jahaṣ was given to the Merarites as a Levitical city (as were Bezer, Heshbon and Kedemoth in Transjordan).[30] Consequently, it is possible to

---

[26] For the Term רית, see the discussion by S. Segert, "Die Sprache der moabitischen Königsinschrift," *Archiv Orientalní* 29/61, p. 244, Donner & Röllig, *KAI* II, p. 175, J. Liver, "The Wars of Mesha, King of Moab," *PEQ* 99/67, p. 24, n. 33.

[27] For Dod as a deity name, see S.R. Driver, *Notes on the Hebrew Text of the Books of Samuel,* Oxford 1890, p. XCI, G.A. Cooke, *A Textbook of North-Semitic Inscriptions,* Oxford 1903, p. 11, Donner & Röllig, *KAI* II, p. 175, G.W. Ahlström, *Psalm* 89, Lund 1959, pp. 164f., A. van den Branden, *Les inscriptions Dédanite,* Beirut 1962, pp. 24, 34, G. Buccellati, *The Amorites in the Ur III Period* (Publicazioni del Seminario di Semitica. Ricerche I), Naples 1966, p. 139, M. Höfner, "Die vorislamischen Religionen Arabiens," in H. Gese – Maria Höfner – Kurt Rudolph, *Die Religionen Alt-syriens, Altarabiens und der Mandäer* (Die Religionen der Menschheit 10/2), Stuttgart 1970, p. 369. Cf. also S.I. Feigin, "The Origin of '*ELOH,* 'God' in Hebrew," *JNES* 3/44, p. 259, F.I. Anderson, "Moabite Syntax," *Orientalia* N.S. 35/66, p. 90, n. 2.

[28] The text does not mention whether Mesha settled Moabites in Nebo, cf. Max Miller, "The Moabite Stone as a Memorial Stela," *PEQ* 106/74, pp. 13f.

[29] According to Eusebius (*Onomasticon* 104:9ff.), Jahaṣ was located between Medeba and Dibon, more specifically, somewhere in the vicinity N. of Dibon, because Mesha says that he annexed Jahaṣ to Dibon. Therefore, Jahaṣ and its territory must have bordered on Dibon's. Y. Aharoni places it further to the north-east of Dibon at Khirbet el-Medeiyineh, *The Land of the Bible,* Philadelphia 1967, p. 306, map 27. C.F. Burney, among others, locates it in the vicinity of Dibon, *The Book of Judges,* London 1918, p. 313, cf. also the discussion below.

[30] One should note that if Omri or Ahab built Jahaṣ, the two passages – Josh. 21:36 and I. Chr. 6:78 – are of no historical value for a reconstruction of the settlement of the Israelites in the 13th and 12th centuries B.C. Moreover, Numbers 32:3 must be seen as a retrojection. For the Moses-Joshua-Conquest theme as a literary fiction, see Ahlström, "Another Moses Tradition," *JNES* 39/80, pp. 65ff.

associate them with the city's cult place.[31] Just as the priests in Egyptian (border) temples, or temples in occupied territories, were royal officials,[32] so the Levites of Jahaṣ, like those of other "Levitical cities", may have been an arm of the royal administration. In the case of Jahaṣ, that would be the northern kingdom, Israel. If this thesis is correct, the Levites must be seen as state employees (more about this below).[33]

In order to strengthen his position in the enlarged kingdom, Mesha not only built or rebuilt cities, he also ordered cisterns to be dug and highways to be constructed. Israelite prisoners of war, among others, were used for these projects (ll. 25f.). Among the cities (re)built by Mesha were Baal-Meon, Qaryaton (ll. 9 ff.) and Aroer (l. 26).[34] In addition, he built the house of Medeba, the house of Diblaton, and the house of Baal-Meon (ll. 30f.). The term בית, "house" in front of these place names may refer to the temples of these cities (בית being the common Canaanite and West-Semitic designation for temple). This conclusion is supported by the fact that in line 9, Baal-Meon occurs as the name of the city. Therefore, the phrase *beth* Baal-Meon is the house (temple) of the city of Baal-Meon.[35] The temples built by the king in these cities should be understood as royal sanctuaries and, as such, part of the state administration. Such building activity must be seen as part of the king's policy of incorporating the conquered areas into his kingdom.[36]

---

[31] M. Haran's thesis that the Levites only lived in the "Levitical" cities (*Temples and Temple Service in Ancient Israel,* Oxford 1978, pp. 116ff.) is rather unconvincing.

[32] W. Helck, *Die Beziehungen Ägyptens zu Vorderasien im 3. und 2. Jahrtausend v. Chr.,* p. 17. According to W.F. Edgerton, groups of civil servants, priests and army officers "overlapped more or less" and were "by no means mutually exclusive," "The Government and the Governed in the Egyptian Empire," *JNES* 6/47, p. 152. Cf. E. Otto, *Ägypten. Der Weg der Pharaonenreiches,* Stuttgart 1958, p. 156.

[33] See below, Chapter IV.

[34] In the excavations at Aroer, a 50 × 50m square fortress was uncovered, see E. Olávarri, "Fouilles à 'Arô'er sur l'Arnon," *RB* 76/69, pp. 230ff. The fortress was reconstructed by the Moabites and later by the Nabateans. However, its origin goes back to the Early Bronze Age. According to P.W. Lapp, Aroer was not really a city, "it was more like a garrison post," "Palestine in the Early Bronze Age," *Near Eastern Archaeology in the Twentieth Century,* ed. by J.A. Sanders, Garden City, N.Y. 1970, p. 111.

[35] Thus Max Miller, "The Moabite Stone as a Memorial Stela," *PEQ* 106/74, p. 14, cf. F.I. Anderson, "Moabite Syntax," *Orientalia* 35/66, pp. 84,93. The term *bet bāmôt* in line 27 may, therefore, refer to a sanctuary, cf. J. Liver, "The Wars of Mesha, King of Moab," *PEQ* 99/67, p. 17, n. 10. Donner & Röllig identify Beth-Bamoth with Bamoth in Num. 21:19f., and Bamoth-Baal in 22:41 and Josh. 13:17, *KAI* II, p. 178. This also suggests that *bet* is not part of the place name.

[36] Establishing new settlements or rebuilding old ones may have been "a function of royal organized corvee and impressment of prisoners," Alan D. Crown, "Some Factors Relating to Settlement and Urbanization in Ancient Canaan in the Second and First Millennia B.C.," *Abr-Nahrain* 11/71, p. 38. In addition to his estate in the capital, a king usually owned extensive lots of territory in the country where he could settle

The קרחה (*qarḥo, qirḥo*) mentioned in the Mesha inscription can perhaps be equated with the acropolis of the city of Dibon (ll. 3,21 ff.). According to B. Mazar, *qirḥu*, "acropolis," is an Akkadian loan-word.[37] However, A.L. Oppenheim understood the cuneiform *kirḫu* as "neither Akkadian nor Semitic," but maintained that it should be compared with a Hittite phrase to be read *šarazziš gurtaš*,[38] which means the upper city. In that light, he saw *kirḫu* as a walled area (cf. OECT IV 150,IV,6 = *dūru*, "wall"[39]) in the center of a city "containing the temple and probably also the palace."[40] If the connection between *kirḫu* and Mesha's קרחה is correct, it means that the inner walled city of Dibon was this קרחה, acropolis, on the עפל,[41] where Mesha built a sanctuary for Moab's god Chemosh.[42] The phenomenon is all the more interesting because it affords us a glimpse into Ancient Near Eastern city planning. In other words, it may have been common to begin construction with fortifications, administrative buildings and a temple on the highest spot of the chosen area surrounded by a wall. The rest of the city, then, evolved out of, around, or at the side of the acropolis on a lower level, and was similarly enclosed by a wall.[43]

---

prisoners, businessmen, military and cult personnel, see Julia Zabłocka, "Palast und König. Ein Beitrag zu den neuassyrischen Eigentumsverhältnissen," *Altorientalischer Forschungen* 4/76, p. 104.

[37] *Encyclopaedia Biblica* IV (in Hebrew), Jerusalem 1962, col. 923, cf. Bezold–Goetze, "Bollwerk," *Babylonische-Assyrisches Glossar*, Heidelberg 1926, *s.v.*

[38] H. Güterbock (private communication).

[39] I am indebted to Prof. M. Weippert for this reference.

[40] *Ancient Mesopotamia*, pp. 131f., cf. H. Güterbock, *JCS* 10/56, p. 95 III: 33ff., "The Hittite Temple According to Written Sources," *Le Temple et le Culte*, p. 125. – That the Ugaritic *grdš* was derived from the Hittite *kurtaš* (cf. W.F. Albright, "New Canaanite Historical and Mythological Data," *BASOR* 63/36, p. 27, n. 9) has been refuted by A. Goetze, "The City Khalbi and the Khapiru People," *BASOR* 79/40, p. 33, and also by J.C. Greenfield, "Some Glosses on the Keret Epic," *Eretz Israel* 9/69, p. 61.

[41] Cf. M. Noth, "Die Wege der Pharaonenheere in Palästina und Syrien," *ZDPV* 60/37, p. 49 (=Aufsätze II, p. 61). Concerning קרחה A.H. van Zijl suggests the reading קְרֻחֹה or קָרֻחָה, *The Moabites*, Leiden 1960, p. 80.

[42] Cf. J.C.L. Gibson, *Textbook of Syrian Semitic Inscriptions* I, Oxford 1973, p. 78. – The term "the sons of Qorah" would thus be a suitable designation for the priests of such a fortress temple.

[43] Cf. A.L. Oppenheim, *Ancient Mesopotamia*, p. 131. Even if the ground happened to be almost level with the rest of the area chosen for the city, the place of the temple-citadel could be raised and enclosed, as was the case, for instance, at Khafaje and Khorsabad. Compare also the modern Erbil (ancient Arba'ilu) where the mosque is built in the center of the city, as was the temple in ancient times, see H. Frankfort, "Town Planning in Ancient Mesopotamia," *The Town Planning Review* 21/50, pp. 98ff., and fig. 6. See also A. Moortgat, *Altvorderasiatische Malerei*, Berlin 1959, pp. 11f., and B. Hrouda, who says that since Old Babylonian times "wird der Tempel zu ebener Erde noch zusätzlich dadurch von seiner profanen Umwelt abgesetzt, das er auf eine Art Podium gestellt und somit im wahrsten Sinne des Wortes erhöht wird," "Le mobilier

Mesha's capital at Dibon appears to have been a new settlement not preceded by any Late Bronze Age or Early Iron Age city.[44] According to A.D. Tushingham, the first settlement of the excavated area dates to around the "middle of the ninth century B.C.,"[45] which coincides with "the floruit of Mesha — about 840–30 B.C."[46] Thus, it is possible to parallel Mesha's building of Dibon with the phenomenon of creating cities "on virgin soil as new capitals (Kār-Tukultī-Ninurta, Kār-Šulmānašarīdu, Dūr-Šarrukīn)."[47] Omri's purchase of the hill of Shemer[48] for the construction of a capital, Samaria, is another parallel. Did Omri build a temple there? I am inclined to

du Temple," *Le Temple et le Culte*, p. 155. J.A. Gallary sees the origin of walled cities and temples in Sumer as a phenomenon of environmental defense" giving protection from flooding, "Town Planning and Community Structure", *The Legacy of Sumer* (Bibliotheca Mesopotamica IV), Malibu, Cal., 1976, pp. 69-77. It should be noted that, according to Thukydides (VI: 2), the Phoenician settlers on Sicily founded their cities on heights and hillocks close to the sea, cf. M. Noth, "Zum Ursprung der phönikischen Küstenstädte," *Welt des Orients* 1/47, pp. 21ff., Ernst Kirsten, *Die griechische Polis als historisch-geographisches Problem des Mittelmeerraumes* (Colloquium Geographicum, Band 5), Bonn 1956, pp. 48f.

[44] Some sherds from the EB period have been found but no building remains, F.V. Winnett and W.L. Reed, *The Excavations at Dibon (Dībân) in Moab. Part II: The Second Campaign, 1952* (AASOR 36-37), 1964, pp. 13, 15. The excavations were carried out on "the southeastern part of the mound." A.D. Tushingham thinks that if a LB or Iron I town existed, it should be sought "on the higher land further to the north," *The Excavations at Dibon (Dhībân) in Moab. The Third Campaign 1952-53* (AASOR 40), 1972, p. 5. For the probability of several Iron I settlements in the area, it should be mentioned that there is some pottery which may be dated to this period, see, J.A. Sauer (rev. of AASOR 40), *Annual of the Department of Antiquities* (Jordan), 20/75, p. 104. E. Stern connected the pottery with the so-called Midianite pottery found at Timna, *IEJ* 25/75, p. 181. In a temple list from the time of Ramses II, a city *t-b-n-i* is mentioned and has been identified with Dibon, see K.A. Kitchen, "Some New Light on the Asiatic Wars of Rameses II," *JEA* 50/64, pp. 47ff., 55, W. Helck, *Die Beziehungen*, pp. 212, 589, 598. S. Ahituv denies the identification of *t-b-n-i* with Dibon because of the occurrence of the town name *tpn* in a list of Thutmosis III. This town should probably be sought in Galilee, "Did Rameses II conquer Dibon?", *IEJ* 22/72, pp. 141f. The same name occurs as *t3-p-n*[...], in an Amenophis III list. According to E. Edel, because this list mentions names from Alalakh in the north to Dothan in the south, no "Moabite" territory would be included, *Die Ortsnamenlisten aus dem Totentempel Amenophis III* (Bonner Biblische Beiträge 25) Bonn 1966, p. 24. It should be noticed that *t-b-n-i* is written ◊ 𓏏 𓃀 𓈖 ◊ 𓈖 𓈖 and *t-p-n*[...] 𓏏 𓈖, see Edel, p. 24. Thus, one may conclude that they are not identical.

[45] Tushingham, *op. cit.*, p. 15, cf. pp. 23f.

[46] Tushingham, p. 24.

[47] A.L. Oppenheim, *Ancient Mesopotamia*, p. 119. Because the Dhībân excavations were carried out on a small area, one cannot, as yet, draw any definitive conclusions.

[48] B. Mazar suggested that there was a family estate on the hill owned by Shemer, see Y. Aharoni–R. Amiran, "A New Scheme for the Sub-Division of the Iron Age in Palestine." *IEJ* 8/58, p. 179, n. 34. A. Alt maintained that there was no settlement before the time of Omri. The pottery from the Early Iron Age cannot prove the existence of a settlement, "Die Stadtstaat Samaria," *Kleine Schriften* III, 1959, p. 258, n. 3.

18   BUILDING AS A POLITICAL TOOL

answer in the affirmative. Just like any ancient Near Eastern head of state undertaking construction of a new capital, it was one of his duties to plan a sanctuary or temple within the palace complex. An indication that this was the case is Hosea's reference to the calf of Samaria (8:5f.), most probably his designation of Samaria's official cult. Therefore, the sanctuary of the calf of Samaria was different from the temple that king Ahab built for his wife Jezebel. Dedicated to the Tyrian Baal, the latter should be understood as a cult place for the queen and her entourage. That it became a competitor of Israel's official religion is another story. The point being emphasized here is that a palace complex in the nation's capital required a sanctuary, for religion and state could not be separated. Indeed, "religion was the ideological base both for the king's existence and for his policies."[49] From this point of view, A. Alt's suggestion that Omri had a sanctuary in his new capital[50] should be taken seriously.[51]

The Acropolis phenomenon

As mentioned above, the "acropolis" phenomenon was common in connection with building fortified cities and was, therefore, not only limited

[49] G.W. Ahlström, "King Jehu – A Prophet's Mistake," *Scripture in History and Theology* Essays in Honor of J. Coert Rylaarsdam), ed. by A.L. Merrill and T.W. Overholt, Pittsburgh 1977, p. 54, cf. also M.A. Cohen, "In all Fairness to Ahab," *Eretz Israel* 12/75, pp. 90*f. See above, p. 2, cf. also G. Widengren, *Sakrales Königtum im Alten Testament und im Judentum* (Franz Delitzsch-Vorlesungen 1952), Stuttgart 1955, pp. 14ff.

[50] The phrase "the calf of Samaria" does not necessarily refer to the bull idol of Bethel as W.F. Albright, among others, has suggested by reading עגלך as a dual (although this reading is possible, it can also be interpreted as both a singular and a plural; if pl. or dual, it is defectively written), *Archaeology and the Religion of Israel*, Baltimore 1946, p. 160, cf. H.W. Wolff, *Hosea* (BK XIV,1), Neukirchen 1961, pp. 179f. The structure of Hos. 8:4–6, with the phrase עגל שמרון in v. 6, shows that עגלך in v. 5 must be singular. The prophet starts with the idols of the nation Israel, and from there he moves towards the center and the god of the capital. For this type of poetic structure, cf. Ahlström, *Psalm 89*, Lund 1959, p. 91. One cannot simply state, on the basis of I Kings 12, that there were only two bull idols (and two temples) in Israel, namely, Bethel and Dan. The Judean "historiographer's" concern was not with statistics. His aim was to discredit the rival cult at Bethel. It should be noted that Hos. 8:4ff. deals with a nation that should not have existed. This is clear from the phrase, "they made kings, but not through me" (v. 4), and its parallel, "with their silver and gold they made idols for themselves." In other words, state and religion were completely wrong because they were not a part of the Davidic establishment with its Yahweh of Jerusalem. Thus, the Hosea passage contains information about Israel's religion, the god of the capital and all the other gods of the country – information that the Judean writer of Hosea used in his propaganda against the northern kingdom. It should be added that מ־ in כי מישראל והוא in v. 6 should be seen as the interrogative מה, according to H.S. Nyberg, who translates: "Denn was hat Israel mit ihm (dem Kalb) zu tun?" *Studien zum Hoseabuche* (Uppsala Universitets Årsskrift 1935:6). Uppsala 1935, p. 62.

to national capitals. Some of the place names in the Old Testament may reflect this custom. For instance, the name of the south-Palestinian city Adoraim may indicate that it consisted of an upper and a lower city or, a "double" city built on two geographical "humps".[52] As early as 1876, J. Fürst understood the dual form to refer to a "Doppelstadt", i.e. an upper and a lower city; the upper city having been constructed first.[53] According to 2 Chr. 11:9, Adoraim was one of the cities fortified (or built) by king Rehoboam of Judah. Another city fortified by the same king was Azekah, usually identified with Tell Zakariya. Excavations at this tell have unearthed an acropolis with a large fortress.[54]

The city of Ramathaim, Samuel's birth place (1 Sam. 1:1), may be another example of this phenomenon.[55] Its sanctuary could have been located either on one of its heights or on a hill in the midst of the city and enclosed by a wall.[56] This city seems to be the one to which the narrator refers in 1 Sam. 9:6. In this text Saul and his *na'ar*, "knight, attendant," come to the land of Zuph where Ramathaim is located. The *na'ar* discloses that a "seer" lives in a nearby town. Although he does not mention his name, in 9:14, this seer is identified with Samuel. It has often been argued

---

[51] "Der Stadtstaat Samaria," *Kleine Schriften* III, 1959, pp. 274ff. G. Wallis considers the "Echtheit" of Hos. 8:5f. as dubious, "Jerusalem und Samaria als Königsstädte," *VT* 26/76, p. 490. See also below, p. 61f.

[52] For a discussion of the root אדר, see Ahlström, *VT* 17/67, pp. 1-7. In I Macc. 13:20 the city is called Adora. It has been identified with Dūrā, ca. 8 km. SW of Hebron, J. Simons, *The Geographical and Topographical Texts of the Old Testament*, Leiden 1959, p. 369. For a discussion about the name, see W. Borée, *Die alten Ortsnamen Palästinas*, Hildesheim ²1968, pp. 55ff., C. Fontinoy, "Les noms de lieux en -*ayin* dans la Bible," *UF* 3, 1971, pp. 39f., M. Görg, *Untersuchungen zur hieroglyphischen Wiedergabe palästinischer Ortsname* (Bonner Orientalische Studien, N.S. 29), Bonn 1971, pp. 3ff. For variant forms of -*ân*, -*ôn*, -*aim*, -*ain*, -*âm*, see also H. Tadmor, "The Campaigns of Sargon II of Assur: A Chronological-Historical Study," *JCS* 12/58, p. 40.

[53] *Hebräisches und chaldäisches Handwörterbuch zum Alten Testament*, Leipzig 1876, *s.v.*

[54] F.J. Bliss and R.A.S. Macalister, *Excavations in Palestine during the years 1898–1900*, London 1902, pp. 12ff. and plate 3. E. Stern dated the fortress of Azekah to no earlier than the eight century B.C., "Azekah," *EAEHL* I, Jerusalem 1975, pp. 141ff. An inscription – most probably – by Sennacherib testifies to the impressive fortifications at Azekah, see N. Na'aman, "Sennacherib's 'Letter to God' on his Campaign to Judah," *BASOR* 21/74, pp. 25ff. The so called Azekah-fragment (BM 82-3-23, 131) has by Na'aman been seen as being a part of text K 6205. H. Tadmor ascribed the Azekah-fragment to Sargon II, *JCS* 12/58, pp. 80ff.

[55] According to Y. Aharoni, this name has a sufformative and not a dual ending, *The Land of the Bible*, p. 109.

[56] For the sanctuary, the *bāmāh*, being located inside the city wall, see W.B. Barrick, *The Word BMH in the Old Testament* (Unpubl. Ph. D. Diss., University of Chicago 1977), pp. 287ff. Note, for instance, that in Am. 7:9 *bāmôt* and *miqdēšē* are parallel terms.

that the narrator of chapter 9 has used folkloristic motifs to tell his story,[57] namely, how a young man, Saul, "unsuspectingly" became king. In a sense this seems to be correct, but the point to be emphasized is that Saul was divinely chosen – in accordance with the Near Eastern royal ideology – and appointed *nāgîd* before he was actually enthroned.[58] The mediator of the divine choice was to be Samuel.[59]

If indeed the name Ramathaim means "the two heights", the discrepancy[60] between 1 Sam. 9:14b and 9:18 disappears (if the text refers to Ramathaim). In v. 14b, when Saul and his knight enter the city, they see Samuel coming towards them in order to go to the *bāmāh*. According to v. 18, Saul approached Samuel "in the gate." This may refer not to the city gate but to the gate leading up to the height where the *bāmāh* was located. Consequently, all three – Samuel, Saul and his knight – were inside the city wall and met at the gate leading up to the *bāmāh*.[61] This is also clear from the following; when the cult feast and its sacrificial meal were over,[62] the participants went down from the *bāmāh* but were still within the city limits, העיר, v. 25.[63]

The acropolis phenomenon may also help us to understand 1 Sam. 10:5ff. Here Samuel told Saul that on his way home he would meet ecstatic prophets in *gibʿeat hāʾĕlohîm* who were descending from the *bāmāh*, the sanctuary, of the city. Both this verse and verse 13, suggest that the *bāmāh*

---

[57] For chapter 9 showing folkloristic motifs, see H. Gressmann, *Die älteste Geschichtsschreibung und Prophetie Israels von Samuel bis Amos und Hosea* (Schriften des Alten Testaments II:1), Göttingen 1921, pp. 26ff., cf. Ivar Hylander, *Die literarische Samuel-Saul-Komplex (1. Sam. 1–15) traditionsgeschichtlich untersucht*, Uppsala und Leipzig 1932, p. 146, Ludwig Schmidt, *Menschlicher Erfolg und Jahwes Initiative* (WMANT 38) Neukirchen 1970, p. 79, B.C. Birch, *The Rise of the Israelite Monarchy: The Growth and Development of I Samuel 7–15* (SBL Diss. Series 27), Missoula, Mont. 1976, pp. 33ff., A.D.H. Mayes, "The Rise of the Israelite Monarchy," *ZAW* 90/78, pp. 13ff.

[58] Cf. B.C. Birch, *op. cit.*, p. 38, T. Mettinger, *King and Messiah* (Coniectanea Biblica, Old Test. Series 8), Lund 1976, pp. 70ff.

[59] That the Deuteronomist was "forced" ideologically to accept Saul's divine election, see R.E. Clements, "The Deuteronomistic Interpretation of the Founding of the Monarchy in I. Sam. VIII," *VT* 24/74, pp. 407f.

[60] Ludwig Schmidt, for example, considers verses 14b and 18 as being written by different hands, *Menschlicher Erfolg und Jahwes Initiative*, p. 72, M. Haran, on the other hand, says that there "is no convincing reason to doubt the homogeneity and continuity of the narrative in 1 Sam. 9," *Temples and Temple Service in Ancient Israel*, Oxford 1978, p. 311, n. 35.

[61] Verse 13 may also indicate that the *bāmāh* was inside the city.

[62] Called a coronation banquet by L. Schmidt, *op. cit.*, pp. 84f.

[63] According to M. Haran, the thirty men invited to the feast were the heads of the families of the city, "Zebah hayyamim," *VT* 19/69, pp. 17f. It is possible that these men were the elders of the town and that Samuel acted as their leader, *ḥazannu* ("mayor"), to use an Akkadian word, cf. the discussion below, pp. 22f.

is inside the city, cf. 1 Chr. 16:39, 21:29. When Saul reached this city, which was probably his home town,[64] he entered its sanctuary ויבא הבמה,[65] and was asked by his *dwd* where he and his נער, knight, had been. Saul told him about the search for the she-asses, revealing only that they had been found. Who, then, is this *dwd*? One must first recognize that, according to 10:5, the city had a Philistine garrison.[66] If this city is Gibeon, from a geographical point of view, it would be an ideal location for the Philistine occupation forces to station a command post.[67] Consequently, the *dwd* may have been an official in the service of the Philistines whose duty it was to keep an eye on the goings on there. Indeed, if this is the case, that Saul did not tell the *dwd* about his designation to kingship is totally understandable. As a Philistine official, this man, even if he was one of Saul's relatives,[68] could quickly have destroyed both Saul and his dreams about kingship.[69] Here the narrator utilized known facts of life from this period, namely, the Philistine occupation. It was his intention to show that Saul was divinely appointed to kingship[70] before he embarked upon his military career. To do so he wrapped his story in the guise of folklore, depicting Saul as a future savior whose election to kingship, willed by the deity, had to be kept a secret so that the oppressors, the Philistines, would not learn of it. In this way, the composition gives an aura of latent drama.

---

[64] Cf. A. Demsky, "Geba, Gibeah, and Gibeon," *BASOR* 212/73, pp. 26ff. It should be noted that the people of the city knew Saul and his family very well, I Sam. 10:11 f. For Saul and the Saulidic family's Gibeonite connections, see J. Blenkinsopp, *Gibeon and Israel* (Society for Old Testament Study 2), Cambridge 1972, pp. 58ff.

[65] L. Schmidt maintains that the phrase "and he entered the *bāmāh*," 10:13, cannot be the "ursprüngliche Wortlaut". Following several other scholars, he changes the text to read ויעל instead of ויבא, *Menschlicher Erfolg und Jahwes Initiative*, p. 115. It should be emphasized that the Hebrew textual tradition is unanimous. No MS has ויעל. Thus, Schmidt interprets a text that does not exist, as far as we know.

[66] The נצבי of the MT may be a misspelling of נציב, cf. I. Sam. 13:3. I Sam. 13: 19ff. tells us that the Philistines kept an eye on everything in order to prevent an uprising against them.

[67] I. Hylander maintained that Saul later tried to make Gibeon his capital, *Der literarische Samuel-Saul-Komplex*, p. 262, cf. also the discussion by J. Blenkinsopp, *Gibeon and Israel*, pp. 68ff., cf. *VT* 24/74, pp. 1ff.

[68] According to Josephus, this *dwd* was Abner who later became Saul's generalissimus, *Antiquities*, Book Six, Chapter 4, cf. I. Sam. 14:50.

[69] P.R. Ackroyd considers the *dwd* to be "an official at the shrine to which Saul went," *The First Book of Samuel* (The Cambridge Bible Commentary, New English Bible), Cambridge 1971, p. 86. D.R. Ap-Thomas maintained that the *dwd* was a Philistine official, "Saul's Uncle," *VT* 11/61, pp. 241ff. If this man was the "governor" of the city it would be quite natural for Saul to meet him in or at the *bāmāh* since it was located within the acropolis of the city and, thus, part of the administrative center.

[70] For the stylistic pattern of the call in this text as well as in Ex. 3:1ff., Judg. 6:11ff., and the call of some of the prophets, see H.H. Schmid, *Der sogennante Yahwist. Beobachtungen und Fragen zur Pentateuchforschung*, Zürich 1976, pp. 19f.

In discussing the phenomenon of sanctuaries as local centers of administration, the information given in 1 Sam. 7:15ff. is important. From this passage we learn of Samuel's yearly visits to Gilgal, Bethel and Mizpah. At the sanctuaries of these places (המקומות, v. 16)[71] he is said to have "judged", שפט, i.e. governed, ruled,[72] the people who, in the Hebrew text are called Israel, את־ישראל.[73] Together with Ramah, Samuel's city of residence, these three places were probably the important administrative and cult centers of the area over which Samuel ruled. There he carried out administrative duties and "reestablished" the religious order of the society year by year.[74] In all probability, his area of jurisdiction did not extend beyond these towns and their immediate surroundings. In other words, his rulership was limited to the central hill country.

The exercize of power in a city (and its surrounding district) was very much in the hands of the city elders.[75] In the Ugaritic rural community, for example, the most prominent of the elders was the ḫazannu,[76] an Akkadian

---

[71] For מקום as a frequent cult-place designation, see F.F. Hvidberg, "The Canaanite Background of Gen. I-III," *VT* 10/60, pp. 285ff., S. Talmon, "Synonymous Readings in the Textual Traditions of the Old Testament," *Scripta Hierosolymitana* VIII, Jerusalem 1961, pp. 359f., M. Weinfeld, *Deuteronomy and the Deuteronomic School,* Oxford 1972, p. 236, n. 3. It should be added that the LXX translates the term in v. 16 with ʾηγιασμένοις.

[72] The term שפט refers to all the duties of a ruler, cf. I. Sam. 8:20 where it is linked with יצא expressing the idea of the ruler leading the people in war.

[73] Cf. C.H.J. de Geus, *The Tribes of Israel,* p. 60. Here we should also note that Samuel (I Sam. 7:13) was adorned with the same laurels as Saul and David, cf. H. Gressmann, *Die älteste Geschichtsschreibung und Prophetie Israels* (Die Schriften des Alten Testaments II:1), Göttingen ²1921, p. 26. In this passage, the cities taken from Israel by the Philistines are said to have been restored to her. However, since Israel as a nation did not exist at that time, no cities could be given back to it. The text is written from the viewpoint of a later time. A Weiser believes this to be the time of David, *Samuel. Seine geschichtliche Aufgabe und religiöse Bedeutung* (FRLANT 81), Göttingen 1962, pp. 22f., Id. "Samuels Philister-Sieg," *ZThK* 56/59, pp. 253ff. See also, J. Blenkinsopp, *Gibeon and Israel,* p. 79. T. Mettinger believes that I Sam. 7:7–14 "presupposes David's subjection of the Philistines," *King and Messiah,* p. 92. However, I Sam. 12:11 underscores that one cannot completely dismiss Samuel as having been a "savior" from oppression.

[74] As a parallel it should be mentioned that the Hittite king and queen as well as members of their court journeyed to annual festivals at different temples, H. Otten, "Götterreisen. B. Nach hethitischen Texten," *Reallexikon der Assyriologie und vorderasiatischen Archäologie,"* Berlin 1969, p. 483. D.A. McKenzie assumes that Samuel, in his younger years, "had gone on a much more extensive circuit", "The Judge of Israel," *VT* 17/67, p. 121. This is, of course, nothing more than pure conjecture.

[75] Cf. H. Klengel, "Die Rolle der 'Ältesten' (LUMEŠŠU.GI) im Kleinasien der Hethiterzeit," *ZA* 57/65, pp. 235f. The elders seem to have had both civil and religious duties, cf. G.W. Ahlström, *Joel and the Temple Cult of Jerusalem* (SVT 21), Leiden 1971, pp. 35f.

[76] M. Helzer, *The Rural Community in Ancient Ugarit,* Wiesbaden 1976, pp. 80ff.

word (cf. *CAD*) which may be translated "chief magistrate of a town"; in other words "mayor" or "Bürgermeister,"[77] "Ortsvorsteher."[78] This title, which is identical to *rabi'ānum, rabânu(m)*, "the great one", is also known from Mari (ARM III:73:9) and Alalakh where it occurs, for instance, in context with the elders.[79] In the Amarna letters it is often used to refer to the ruler of a city-state.[80] This is quite natural, since a city ruler could not call himself a king when writing to the Pharaoh. It may, perhaps, be possible to compare *ḫazannu/rabânu* with the Canaanite *šōpēṭ* or *šar*, both of which are found in the Old Testament. In Assyria and Babylonia, the *ḫazannu* was a city leader usually appointed by the king. According to H.W.F. Saggs, in Babylonia his status was "as much religious as civil."[81] This may be explained by the fact that religion was a collective phenomenon and, as such, was community business.

With this as a background, it is tempting to see Samuel as a city leader of the Syro-Palestinian *ḫazannu/rabânu-šōpēṭ* type whose influence extended to other places outside his own city. To judge from the tradition in I Sam. 12:11, Samuel was an important leader to the residents of the central hill country. This text states that Samuel was one of the four men of the premonarchic time who saved the people from oppression. The three others were Jerubbaal, Bedan and Jephtah.[82] It appears that certain groups of people remembered Samuel as a hero. Later tradition built him up as a leader of all the Israelites and, as a consequence, the biblical historiographer arranged him among the "judges" and made him a prophetic spokesman for Deuteronomistic ideas. If, as the biblical tradition maintains, he was educated as a priest, he may be characterized as a priest ruler. This may be the basis for perceiving him as a prophet since priests sometimes fulfilled prophetic duties.[83]

Two other examples of local hill country leaders may be mentioned. The

---

[77] Cf. N.B. Jankowska, "Communal Self-Government and the King of the State of Arrapha," *JESHO* 12/69, pp. 265ff.

[78] H. Klengel, "Zu den *šībūtum* in altbabylonischer Zeit", *Orientalia* 29/60, pp. 371f.

[79] D.J. Wiseman, *The Alalakh Tablets*, 1953, text 2, 27, cf. p. 158b (Index).

[80] Cf. H.J. Katzenstein, *The History of Tyre,* Jerusalem 1973, p. 31. Cf. G. Buccellati, *Cities and Nations of Ancient Syria* (Studi Semitici 26), Rome 1967, pp. 65ff. For the *ḫazannu* of Gezer (occurring on a 7th century Akkadian inscription, R.A.S. Macalister, *The Excavations of Gezer* I, London 1911, pp. 22ff.), see, for instance, R. Giveon, "An Egyptian Official at Gezer," *IEJ* 22/72, pp. 143f.

[81] *The Greatness that was Babylon,* New York 1963, p. 252.

[82] For this tradition which does not know anything about a Joshua "conquest", see Ahlström, "Another Moses Tradition," *JNES* 39/80, pp. 65ff. Because this text knows of only four leaders or "saviors", it may originate from a time before the Deuteronomic reconstruction of the history which occurs in the book of Judges.

[83] G.W. Ahlström, "Prophecy," *Encyclopaedia Britannica*, 15th ed. 1974, *s.v.*

head priest of Shiloh, Eli, should also be seen as a priest-ruler if the textual material about him reflects history. Eli was probably of Canaanite origin – a priest of the god 'Alu.[84] As a leader of a central Israelite district, he was included among the "judges" by the later historiographer (I Sam. 4:18) who, quite possibly, had recourse to old traditions about the country's heroes. Consequently, the story about Eli and the Israelites worshipping at Shiloh may provide interesting hints about the real history of the hill country in pre-monarchic time. The majority of people around Shiloh may have been of Canaanite origin. Dwelling close to the Israelites who lived between Shechem and Shiloh, they were later counted as belonging to them.[85] We should also note that Eli is not given any ancestry in the book of Samuel. However, in I Chr. 24:3, like all priests who were "Israelitized", he was connected with the "tribe" of Levi as an Aaronide of the line of Ithamar[86] (2 Esdr. 1:2f. associates him with the line of Eleazar).

Judges 17 relates that a man, Micah, built a temple, made idols for it and installed one of his sons as its priest. This indicates that Micah was no ordinary farmer since building temples and appointing priests were royal prerogatives. Later Micah is said to have appointed a Levite as the main priest in the temple. Supporting the theory that Micah was a city ruler or petty prince, one should note that when he was robbed of his Levite and idols by the Danites, he pursued them with his men in order to recover his property. This is military business. When Micah realized that his troops were not as strong as those of the Danites, he returned home.[87]

Finally, one more observation is necessary. Because Palestinian archae-

---

[84] See H.S. Nyberg, "Studien zum Religionskampf im Alten Testament," *ARW* 35/ 38, pp. 329ff. For a discussion about *'al* as an epithet of Yahweh, cf. L. Viganò, *Nomi e titoli di YHWH alla luce del semitico del Nord-ovest* (Biblica et Orientalia 31), Rome 1976, pp. 34ff.

[85] For the settlement problems of the central hill country, see my article, "Another Moses Tradition," pp. 65ff.

[86] According to F.M. Cross, this statement is "based on a reordering of the genealogies and cannot be taken at face value," *Canaanite Myth and Hebrew Epic,* Cambridge, Mass., 1973, p. 207, n. 50. Cross sees the Eli clan as being Mushite, pp. 195ff. Because in the Old Testament construction of history, Shiloh is mentioned as the place where Yahweh first made his name "dwell" (Jer. 7:12) after the "conquest", it is natural that the head priest of its temple be associated with the "tribe" of Levi.

[87] G.W. Ahlström, *Aspects of Syncretism in Israelite Religion,* p. 25. As to the problems of composition, see, for instance, M. Noth, "The Background of Judges 17-18", *Israel's Prophetic Heritage,* ed. by B.W. Anderson, and W. Harrelson, New York 1962, pp. 68ff. Concerning the historical traditions in Judg. 17-18 where no "Judge" is mentioned (probably because the narrator's pattern did not fit his material), R.G. Boling assumes that "by the mid-eleventh century they [the Judges] were probably quite ineffective and increasingly corrupt."(!), *Judges* (Anchor Bible 6A), Garden City, N.Y., 1975, p. 23. This would be a logical conclusion only if one accepts the narrator's historiographic pattern as the historical fact.

ology has been primarily "tell minded", we have relatively little knowledge about the areas around the ancient cities even though several surveys have been undertaken during the last decades. We do not know, for instance, whether the villages, *bānôt*, governed by a city had any sanctuaries or cult places. Although it was not necessary to place cultic and military personnel in these villages, several, if not all of the villages, may have had their own cultplaces as was the case in the Ugaritic kingdom.[88] There the communal rites such as harvest rituals were performed. These were probably acted out at the site, for example, at threshing floors and winepresses.[89] If this was the case, these villages had their own cultic functionaries, just as in the kingdom of Ugarit.[90] Such a functionary could have been the leading elder of the community who, like the *ḫazannu*, had cultic duties. However, one should caution against making too sharp a distinction between priests and laymen. The leader of a community, be it a state or a village, was the leader of the society's actions.

---

[88] M. Helzer, *The Rural Community in Ancient Ugarit*, Wiesbaden 1976, pp. 71ff.

[89] Cf. G.W. Ahlström, "Der Prophet Nathan und der Tempelbau," *VT* 11/61, pp. 115ff., *Joel and the Temple Cult of Jerusalem*, p. 111. For winepresses in the area around Ta'anak, see my article, "Winepresses and Cup-Marks of the Jenin-Megiddo Survey," *BASOR* 231/78, pp. 19–49. For Greece, see, for instance, M.P. Nilsson, *Griechische Feste von religiöser Bedeutung mit Ausschluss der Attischen*, Leipzig 1906, pp. 331f. In objecting to *gōren*, threshing floor, as being used for harvest rituals, H.H. Rowley understood the information in 2 Sam. 24:25, that David built an altar on the threshing floor of Araunah, as proof that this was a non-sacral site. It became holy only with the construction of the Yahweh altar, *Worship in Israel*, Philadelphia 1967, p. 77, n. 2, cf. also G. Münderlein, *ThWAT* II (1974), 1977, cols. 69f. On the other hand, one could refute this by saying that because Araunah's threshing floor had the nimbus of sacrality, a Yahweh altar could be built on it. Had the place not been sacred it would, of course, have been a profanation to built an altar there. F.M. Cross mis understood the idea of the *gōren* as a sometime cultplace when he stated that the "*king* of Jerusalem was not *threshing* in his sanctuary," *Canaanite Myth and Hebrew Epic*, p. 210, n. 58. Cross did not understand the connection and relationship between harvest and ritual. He supports his opinion by theorizing that the text is corrupt. Cf. also V. Fritz, *Tempel und Zelt*, Neukirchen 1977, pp. 17f. However, to use, as Cross does, the Chronicler's version (I Chr. 21:21) and the 4QSam^a text in order to rewrite the story of 2 Sam. 24:23a is a dubious method. Cf. Cross, "The History of the Biblical Text in Light of Discoveries in the Judean Desert," *HTR* 57/64, pp. 294f. It should be mentioned that there are no textual problems in 2 Sam. 24:23a. The Masoretic tradition is unanimous and the versions support it. Rather, the problem comes after v. 23a, where it is possible to see a gap in the text. Although my concern is not with Araunah's (Ornan's) activities, if indeed, he was threshing wheat, as the Chronicler says, this phenomenon was a ritual one. Cross' reconstruction of the text is misleading. The "routine haplography by homoioarkton" refers to, as he notes, 2 Sam. 24:20 (the MT has מלך and the text in I Chr. 21:20f. מלאך; the one who writes *mal'āk* instead of *melek* is probably a "pious" interpreter) and *not* to 2 Sam. 24:23a. The Chronicler's version which makes an "angelic" story out of the meeting between the two kings cannot be considered to have historical priority.

[90] M. Helzer, *op. cit.*, p. 73.

Popular religion

The existence of communal rites and feasts makes it possible to draw a conclusion which is of some importance for the study of religion in the ancient Near East. The rituals of a village may be characterized as "popular" religion — a term often used but never defined with regard to content in the cultures of the Near East. These local rituals were not part of the official, national religion, which was directed from the capital by the king's administration. However, popular and national religion may have mutually influenced each other at certain times and, therefore, ressemblances are to be expected. Indeed, it is probable that royal actions in religious matters resulted in interference in the popular religion. On the other hand, there were times when the national religion received new directives through royal edicts that did not essentially alter the rituals and beliefs of the villages. Whether, for example, king Josiah's reorganization of his administration and national religion affected communal religion is impossible to determine since no information about the problem is available. What we do know is that Josiah's reform was of some consequence for the national sanctuaries, 2 Kings 23:5. Some priests, appointed by the kings of Judah, were deposed. Consequently, it can be maintained that the Judahite village festivals continued as before. Because they were, in the main, directed to (the) fertility gods, Josiah's order that only in Jerusalem could sacrifice be directed to Yahweh may not have changed much, if anything, of the rural communities' religious life. It should also be remembered that the king could not easily alter agricultural customs.

CHAPTER THREE

ADMINISTRATION AND BUILDING ACTIVITIES
IN THE DAVIDIC-SOLOMONIC KINGDOM

Exactly how the nation was administered during the reigns of Saul and David is not made clear by the texts. It is particularly the administrative organization under Saul that escapes us. Of course, he could not have ruled without some administrative personnel. For example, we know that Abner was his שר הצבא, generalissimus, I Sam. 14:50, 17:55.[1] The priest Ahia may have been the chief priest of the new kingdom, 1 Sam. 14:3, 18, and the servants of Saul, mentioned in I Sam. 16:17, 22:6f., 9.14, may have comprised the king's entourage, the court members. However, because the narrators were not interested in how the country was administered, we learn no more about it.

It should not be assumed that the administration of the monarchy of Israel emerged in a vacuum. Instead, it must be remembered that Egypt played an important political role in Palestine.[2] Consequently, it can be maintained that both the administration and the court system of the Canaanite city states were partly influenced by the Egyptian system, at least from the 18th dynasty. From the Tell el-Amarna letters we know that the princes of the Canaanite city states had to send their sons, the presumptive heirs, to Pharoah's court to be 'educated' and so to become faithful vassals.[3] In the Egyptian capital, the Versailles of its time, they learned how court and administration were organized and functioned.[4] In addition, the presence of Egyptian administrators and military personnel in Palestine certainly contributed to the spread of the Egyptian system.

Consequently, it is likely that when Syro-Palestinian petty kings (including the Jerusalemite king) organized their own administrations, they

---

[1] This term is also used in connection with Sisera, Judg. 4:7, and Joab, 1 Kings 1:19, as well as for two Aramean generals, 2 Sam. 10:18, 2 Kings 5:1.

[2] The biblical writers do not spell out the fact that the reign of Solomon (for example) also was a time of Phoenician-Egyptian influence that was, by and large, foreign to the people of the hill country.

[3] See, for instance, EA 171:4 and 296:25-28. The latter says that the prince Iaḫtiri was first sent to the Egyptian court and later was "tested" at the Egyptian base at Azzati (Gaza), cf. J. A. Knudtzon, *Die Tell el-Amarna Tafeln* II, bearbeitet von O. Weber und E. Ebeling, Leipzig 1915 (reprint Aalen 1964), pp. 1275, 1346.

[4] Cf. K.-H. Bernhardt, "Verwaltungspraxis in spätbronzezeitlichen Palästina," *Beiträge zur sozialen Struktur des alten Vorderasien,* Berlin 1971, pp. 133ff.

used the Egyptian system as a model.[5] For instance, the *mazkīr* of Jerusalem which occurs in 2 Sam. 8:16 *et passim* may have as its counterpart the Egyptian *whm.w*, "Sprecher, Mitteiler", i.e. speaker, spokesman, herald.[6] Another title which appears in the abovementioned passage is *sōphēr*. Its Egyptian parallel is the *sš nsw*, "royal scribe", which seems to have been a common title referring not only to the Pharoah's chief scribe.[7] Another title for a high official is the "king's friend" (רעה) of Gen. 26:26, Jer. 52:25, which also is known from the el-Amarna letters, [lú]*ruḫi šarri*, EA 228:11.[8] In the case of David, it is highly probable that his military and court system were fashioned both upon the Egyptian example and Jebusite administrative practice.[9] His top government officials are listed in 2 Sam. 8:16-18 and 20: 23-26, cf. I Chr. 18:15-17. If J. Begrich's reconstruction of the first list is correct,[10] the high officials in order of rank would be: Joab (over the army), Seraiah (the *sōphēr*), Jehoshaphat (the *mazkīr*), Benaiah (over the Cherethites and Pelethites), Zadoq (the priest) and David's sons (priests). In the second list, the order is different: Joab (over the army), Benaiah (over the Cherethites and the Pelethites), Adoram (Adoniram of I Kings 4:6f.; 5:28, over forced labor), Jehoshaphat (*mazkīr*), Sheya (*sōphēr*), Zadoq and Abia-

---

5 Cf. A. Cody, *A History of the Old Testament Priesthood* (Analecta Biblica 35), Rome 1969, pp. 96f.

6 J. Begrich, "Sōphēr und Mazkīr. Ein Beitrag zur inneren Geschichte des davidisch-salomonischen Grossreiches und des Königreiches Juda," *ZAW* 58/40-41, pp. 5f. Cf. R. de Vaux, "Titres et functionnaires égyptiens à la cour de David et Salomon," *RB* 48/39, pp. 394ff., S. Herrmann, *A History of Israel in Old Testament Times*, pp. 160f. For the translation of *whm.w*, see A. Erman–H. Grapow, *Wörterbuch der ägyptischen Sprache* I, Leipzig 1926, p. 344. It should be noted that Begrich also saw the "Fron-arbeit" system as being of Egyptian origin, *op. cit.*, p. 11. For a discussion about Egyptian influences in these matters, see also A. Alt, "Neues über Palästina aus dem Archiv Amenophis IV," *Palästinajahrbuch* 20/24, pp. 34ff. (*KS* III, 1959, pp. 169ff.), J.A. Soggin, "The Period of the Judges and the Rise of the Monarchy," in *Israelite and Judean History,* ed. by J.H. Hayes and J.M. Miller (The Old Testament Library), Philadelphia 1977, pp. 356ff.

7 W. Helck compares it with an "academic" degree, *Zur Verwaltung des Mittleren und Neuen Reichs,* Leiden-Cologne 1958, p. 61. Cf. R.J. Williams, "A People Come out of Egypt. An Egyptologist looks at the Old Testament," *SVT* 28/74, pp. 235f. Williams understands the Hebrew *mazkīr* as "chief of protocol," p. 236. For a corresponding title in an Amarna text (316:16) from Yurza (*sš-š 't*, "writer of letters," occurring as *saḫšiḫa*), see W.F. Albright, "Cuneiform Material for Egyptian Prosopography 1500–1200 B.C.," *JNES* 5/46, pp. 20f. It also occurs in the Wen-Amun story, see H. Goedicke, *The Report of Wenamun,* Baltimore and London 1975, p. 119.

8 2 Sam. 15:37, 16:16f., 1 Kings 4:5, 1 Chr. 27:33, cf. Gen. 26:26. See H. Donner, "Der 'Freund des Königs'," *ZAW* 73/61, pp. 269-277.

9 One should note that David did neither destroy Jerusalem nor did he kill its inhabitants when he conquered the city.

10 *ZAW* 58/40-41, pp. 5f.

thar (priests) and David's priest Ira from Jair.[11] The latter is not given any Levitical ancestry which indicates that it was not required in the time of David.

It is possible that the text of 2 Sam. 8:17 is corrupt, as has often been argued.[12] After Zadoq the text mentions Ahimelek ben Abiathar instead of the expected, Abiathar. First it should be stressed that Abiathar's position at David's court is not quite clear, and that perhaps even his name is an insertion. Moreover, both lists of David's top officials have only one name for each office, but when the priestly office is mentioned we find two.[13] This raises the question of whether the second priest name was added by the narrator — Ahimelek ben Abiathar in the first list and Abiathar in the second. Begrich's reconstruction of the first list, which includes only Zadoq's name, seems correct if the list refers to the top officials. However, from the narrator's viewpoint it was astonishing that Abiathar was not given the post as the top ranking official of religious affairs. After all, he was the priest of the pre-Jerusalemite time and represented a tradition older than the Jerusalemite one. From this point of view, Abiathar's inclusion in the second list, 2 Sam. 20:23ff., is understandable. However, he was never the head priest of the Jerusalemite religious establishment — a fact that is not surprising when one considers the possibility that David himself was not an Israelite. Coming from Bethlehem, a city under Jebusite rule and not part of Saul's kingdom,[14] David was perhaps more familiar with the Jebusite administrative apparatus. Consequently, he did not put it out of business when he became king — but he could, however, have reorganized it. It was Zadoq, one of the officials David took over from the Jebusite establishment, who held the reins of religious administration during David's regime. The scholarly idea that Zadoq and Abiathar shared the position of chief priest is unrealistic. That Zadoq was the top ranking priest seems evident from the fact that he is usually mentioned first in the texts, cf. 2 Sam. 15:24ff.[15] As

---

[11] That Ira is called David's priest may indicate that he was not a top official of the royal administration but was David's palace priest.

[12] So recently T. Mettinger, *Solomonic State Officials*, p. 7, F.M. Cross, *Canaanite Myth and Hebrew Epic*, pp. 211ff.

[13] The mention of David's sons as priests may indicate their high position. It was not uncommon at that time for high priestly offices to be given to princes.

[14] David's brothers, mentioned in 1 Sam. 16:6f. (Eliab, Abinadab, and Shammah) have Canaanite names. Moreover, David's own name cannot be labelled as Yahwistic. For David as a non-Israelite, see my article, "Was David a Jebusite Subject?", *ZAW* 92/80, pp. 285ff.

[15] Cf. Ahlström, *VT* 11/61, p. 122. A.R. Carlson maintains that "the Jebusite-Jerusalemite high-priest Zadok occupies a position of prominence in the 'deuteronomized' version of 15:24-29, over against the Israelite 'triumvirate' Abiathar, the Ark and the Levites," *David and Chosen King*, 1964, p. 174. Because of 1 Chr. 16:39 it has been suggested that Zadoq was a Gibeonite, E. Auerbach, "Die Herkunft der Sadokiden," *ZAW* 49/31, pp. 327f. Cf. also M. Noth, "Das deutsche evangelische Institut für Alter-

to the Israelite priest from Nob, Abiathar, it is possible that he was given a prominent and revered position at the court in gratitude for his earlier services to David, and perhaps also in order to appease the people of the north.

Returning again to the two lists of David's officials, it must be stated that it is not necessary to harmonize their differences. Certainly it is conceivable that during David's tenure as king he replaced some administrative personnel. Therefore, the lists may reflect different points in time during his reign. One indication that David either reorganized his administration or appointed additional personnel is the name of the *sōphēr* which is different in the two lists. In the first his name is Seraiah, but in the second, we find the name Sheya.[16]

The occurrence of the name Adoram in the second list, 2 Sam. 20:23 (spelled Hadoram in 2 Chr. 10:18) may be another indication of administrative reshuffling. It is possible that he was of Jebusite descent and belonged to a religious group worshipping Hadad/Adad.[17] Probably late in David's reign he was appointed as chief over the forced labor and he con-

---

tumswissenschaft des Heiligen Landes. Lehrkurs 1956," *ZDPV* 73/57, p. 10. M. Haran suggested that Zadoq came from Hebron, "Studies in the Account of the Levitical Cities II," *JBL* 80/61, p. 161, and so also F.M. Cross, *Canaanite Myth and Hebrew Epic*, pp. 214ff. Cross' argumentation includes a subjective statement, namely, that he cannot understand why David would "invite a pagan priest as one of the high priests of the national cults," p. 210. To this one can object that the term 'pagan' is not applicable to the religions of that time. Moreover, David did not invite anyone to become a priest. A king appoints, and he appoints whomever he wants. When David took Jerusalem, the establishment of the city became nominally Israelite. However, the chief priest of pre-Davidic Jerusalem continued in the same position under the new ruler. It should also be pointed out that David's Yahwism is problematic. David not only attempted "to draw all the old League traditions to his new establishment," as Cross puts it (p. 210) [such a league is, by the way, an unproven hypothesis], but aimed to meld all the different peoples of his kingdom together as a nation. Because religion was one of the most natural means for this, the different religious traditions – both Israelite and Canaanite – became part of the nation's beliefs. Thus, this means that most of them were not in harmony with the later historiographer's ideas. Cross' error is that, in his analysis of the early monarchy, he utilized viewpoints and evaluations about what Yahwism ought to have been that derive from a later time.

[16] A. Cody advocated that Sheya (שיא), as well as שישא, 1 Kings 4:3, and שושא, 1 Chr. 18:16, are corruptions of the Egyptian *sš š.'t* or *sh š'. t*, "Le titre égyptien et le nom propre de scribe de David," *RB* 72/65, pp. 381ff., cf. also T. Mettinger, *Solomonic State Officials*, pp. 25ff., J. Gray, *I & II Kings*, p. 132. R. de Vaux considered not only the office of the *sōphēr* but also the family of scribes as Egyptian, "Titres et functions égyptiens à la cour de David et Salomon," *RB* 48/39, pp. 398ff. However, this denies the possibility of any scribal activity in the Jerusalemite court, Jebusite or Israelite. The Amarna letters from Abdi-Hepa of Jerusalem contradict de Vaux's hypothesis.

[17] Cf. also the Akkadian name Adduramu. For the form Adoniram as being a tendentious rewriting of Adoram, see J.A. Montgomery and H.S. Gehman, *A Critical and Exegetical Commentary on the Books of Kings* (ICC), Edinburg 1951, p. 119, cf. also Mettinger, *op. cit.*, p. 133.

tinued in that position throughout Solomon's tenure. When Rehoboam attempted to bring Israel under the Jerusalemite king's scepter, he was stoned to death, 1 Kings 12:18. This is understandable if Adoram is viewed not only as a representative of the Jerusalemite administration's labor policies but also as a personification of the "Jebusite" rulership of the Davidic dynasty which the north had come to distrust and to feel as foreign.

It should be noted that the corvée system was a well known institution in the Syro-Palestinian world long before the emergence of the nation Israel. It is mentioned in a letter from Ta'anak (No. 2, 15th cent. B.C.),[18] in a letter from Biridiya of Megiddo (Amarna time),[19] in texts from Ugarit,[20] and from Alalakh.[21] From these examples I. Mendelsohn drew the conclusion that even if the instances from Ta'anak and Megiddo show that a foreign power, Egypt, demanded this kind of work of its vassals, it nevertheless "is evident that the Egyptians did not initiate this institution in Palestine. The local Egyptian officials simply continued a practice that had previously been employed by the native governments."[22] Therefore, when David appointed Adoram[23] as the chief administrator over forced labor, 2 Sam. 20:23,[24] he was following a well established pattern.

Solomonic kingdom

When Solomon took over David's administration, he must have enlarged it. Indeed, his district organization, with the building of store cities and

---

[18] W.F. Albright, "A Prince of Ta'anach in the Fifteenth Century B.C.," *BASOR* 94/44, p. 22.

[19] F. Thureau-Dangin, "Nouvelles letters d'el-Amarna," *RA* 19/1922, p. 97. Cf. *ANET* p. 485.

[20] I. Mendelsohn, "On Corvée Labor in Ancient Canaan and Israel," *BASOR* 167/62, pp. 31ff.

[21] A.F. Rainey, "Compulsory Labor Gangs in Ancient Israel," *IEJ* 20/70, pp. 192f. Consult also M. Held, "The Root *ZBL/SBL* in Akkadian, Ugaritic and Biblical Hebrew," *JAOS* 88/68, pp. 90-96.

[22] *BASOR* 167/62, pp. 32f. 1 Sam. 8:11-18 can be understood against this background, cf. I. Mendelsohn, "Samuel's Denunciation of Kingship", *BASOR* 143/56, pp. 103ff.

[23] The problem of whether Saul and David forced the Israelites and Judeans as well as the *gērîm* and the "subjected" Canaanites to do forced labor is, for the time, irrelevant. Here, I am concerned about the existence of the phenomenon. However, the information given in 2 Sam. 12:31 and 1 Chr. 22:2, excusing the Israelites from this kind of duty, may be expressive of a late ideology according to which only captives, foreigners and above all, Canaanites *should* do the dirty work.

[24] J. Gray doubts that the corvée system "was instituted at all under David." However, at the same time he says that in "the Canaanite cities now incorporated into the kingdom of Israel the system had probably been in practice," *I & II Kings,* p. 134. Yes, but what then about Jerusalem?

fortresses, the reorganization of the army and the introduction of chariotry required more official personnel than the kingdom had seen thus far. From this time on we find, for instance, a minister (manager) of the royal palaces and estates called *'ăšer 'al habbayit*, I Kings 4:6.[25] This title is the parallel of the Egyptian *îmy-r₃ pr wr* which literally means "overseer of the house where 'house' has its wide sense of estate."[26] It is commonly translated "high, great steward."[27] Obviously this office continued through the Judean monarchy,[28] 1 Kings 16:9, 18:3, 2 Kings 10:5, 15:5, 18:18, 37, 19:2, and Isa. 22:15.

It had been maintained that Solomon's division of Israel into twelve provinces, I Kings 4,[29] was inspired by Pharoah Shoshenq's administrative system with its levy "arranged in twelve monthly sections.[30] Taking into account the fact that Egypt had long provided the model for the organization of the royal courts of Palestine, such influence is not impossible. However, it is doubtful that the model for the district division was that of Pharoah Shoshenq (945 – ca. 915/13 B.C.). The biblical text does not state exactly when Solomon inaugurated this system, but if it was initiated during, or shortly before he started to build his temple and palace complex (begun in the 4th year of his reign, I Kings 6:1),[31] then his district system was

[25] Cf. J. Gray, *I & II Kings*, p. 133, T.N.D. Mettinger, *Solomonic State Officials*, pp. 70ff. See also W. Helck, *Zur Verwaltung des Mittleren und Neuen Reichs*, pp. 103ff.

[26] A.H. Gardiner, *Ancient Egyptian Onomastica* I, Oxford 1947, pp. 45*ff., cf. Helck, "Verwalter," *op. cit.*, pp. 92f. This kind of title may have been common in the ancient Near East, cf. the Akkadian ˡᵘša muḫḫi bītāni, "the (man) in charge over the house (palace)," see R.P. Dougherty, "Cuneiform Parallels to Solomon's Provisioning System," *AASOR* 5/23-24, p. 31. See also R.J. Williams, "A People Come out of Egypt," *SVT* 28, 1974, pp. 236f.

[27] W.A. Ward, "The Egyptian Office of Joseph," *JSS* 5/60, pp. 146f.

[28] Cf. H.G. May, "The Hebrew Seals and the Status of Exiled Jehoiakin," *AJSL* 56/39, pp. 146ff.

[29] M. Noth, *The History of Israel*, pp. 212ff., G.E. Wright, "The Provinces of Solomon," *Eretz Israel* 8/67, pp. 58*ff. M. Ottosson maintains that 1 Kings 4:19 refers to the time before Solomon, *Gilead. Tradition and History*, Lund 1969, pp. 219f. If so, Geber would be a district governor from the time of David. This would mean that there were other governors in the Davidic kingdom. Considering the fact that several old Canaanite city-states came under the crown of Jerusalem with David, governors as well as military and cultic personnel had to be placed in them. The report about David's census, 2 Sam. 24, may indicate the beginning of a district organization and a basis for taxation of the population, cf. A. Alt, "The Settlement of the Israelites in Palestine," *Essays in Old Testament History and Religion*, Garden City, N.Y., 1967, p. 211. Solomon then reshaped the organization.

[30] D.B. Redford, "Studies in Relations between Palestine and Egypt during the First Millennium B.C.," *Studies in the Ancient Palestinian World*, ed. by J.W. Wevers and D.B. Redford, Toronto 1972, pp. 153ff. Cf. also J. Begrich, *ZAW* 58/40-41, pp. 1-29.

[31] Cf. the discussion by M. Noth, *Könige* (BK IX), p. 110 and by Th. A. Busink, *Der Tempel von Jerusalem* I, p. 589, n. 69.

instituted before the reign of Shoshenq.[32] The levy mentioned in 1 Kings 5:27ff. (Engl. transl. 5:13ff.) is said to have started before the work began on the temple at Jerusalem. It is probable that the levy required the district division.[33] Thus, if Egypt contributed the model for this system, it must have been the genius of Siamon (979–960) or Psusennes II (960–946). Unfortunately, we do not know the regnal years of Solomon (nor those of David). Although he is said to have ruled for forty years, that length of time should not be viewed as reliable. Rather, it equals the span of a generation.[34]

That Solomon's district organization antedates the conception that the people were composed of twelve tribes, is highly probable. The tribal system may represent an historiographical theory about the origin of the different ethnic groups within the united kingdom. As such, it was used to express the totality of the "Israelite" peoples,[35] and was coupled with the late promise of the land to Abraham, the twelve tribal ancestors becoming his grandsons.[36] If this is indeed the case, it is incorrect to assert that Solomon disregarded the tribal system when he organized his kingdom in districts, each headed by a governor.[37] The division of the country was made according to geographical "units".[38] This becomes clear when examining, for example, district five which included the southern part of the Jezreel valley with the cities of Megiddo, Ta'anak, Dothan, Ibleam, and Beth-Shan, plus both sides of the Jordan river valley down to Adam. This area consists of lowlands, plains and valleys which hang together geographically and thus economically. On the *ghōr*, or east side of the Jordan, the road called "the way of the plain" (2 Sam. 18:23) met the road from Megiddo opposite

---

[32] See A.R. Green, who thinks that Jeroboam possibly influenced Shoshenq in this matter, "Israelite Influence at Shishak's Court?", *BASOR* 233/79, pp. 59-62.

[33] According to Y. Aharoni, the purpose of the district organization was "to improve the efficiency and intensity of tax collection", *The Land of the Bible*, p. 277.

[34] For the chronology of the Israelite and Judean Kings, see the discussion by J.M. Miller in Hayes and Miller, *Israelite and Judean History*, p. 682.

[35] Cf. C.H.J. de Geus, *The Tribes of Israel*, p. 117. Note the information given about the Arameans descending from twelve ancestors, Gen. 22:20f., and the Arabs (Ishmael and his twelve sons), Gen. 25:23ff., and Edom (Esau and his twelve sons), Gen. 36:10ff. These texts cannot refer to the MB II period. Becasue of the inclusion of the Arabs they may be from the time after ca. 800 B.C., cf. J. van Seters, *Abraham in History and Tradition*, pp. 59f.

[36] For the promise of the land, see W.M. Clark, *The Origin and Development of the Land Promise Theme in the Old Testament* (Diss. Yale Univ. 1964), pp. 61ff., cf. also J. van Seters, *op. cit.*, pp. 249ff., 264. Thomas L. Thompson dates the patriarchal stories to the Iron Age period, *The Historicity of the Patriarchal Narratives* (BZAW 133), Berlin 1974, pp. 325f.

[37] Contra J. Wellhausen, *Prolegomena to the History of Ancient Israel* (Meridan Books), Cleveland, Ohio, 1957, p. 456, G.E. Wright, "The Provinces of Solomon," *Eretz Israel* 8/67, p. 59*, and T.N.D. Mettinger, *Solomonic State Officials*, p. 119.

[38] "Political units are far more coincident with geographical areas," C.H.J. de Geus, *The Tribes of Israel*, p. 138.

Beth-Shan. The road on the eastern side of the river seems to have been more important than the road on the western because of the large number of settlements on the eastern side.[39] It should be noted that the river did not really separate the two sides as did the Jordan plateau since there were many accessible fords.[40] In antiquity, it was not rivers and straits that divided people, but mountains and heavily forrested areas.[41]

In passing it should be mentioned that it took approximately thirteen years to complete the palace and seven years to build the temple. That the royal palace complex took that long reveals something about its size when compared with the size of the temple. It is no wonder that a district organization including the levy and corvée became necessary. If Solomon wanted to build something on the grand scale of the Pharoahs, one could, of course, assume that his palace and temple complex were Egyptian inspired. However, it has usually been maintained that the temple represented a common Syrian or Phoenician type of architecture,[42] because of the Tyrian workers employed by Solomon, I Kings 7:13ff. It has been suggested that the palace was an exponent of the *bīt-ḥilāni* type[43] and that the temple was modelled on the Syrian temple at Tell Taʿyīnāt.[44] However, this temple is later than the Solomonic one (9th c. B.C.).[45] Moreover, even though there are similarities, there are also notable differences,[46] particularly the fact that the Tell Taʿyīnāt temple contained only two rooms while Solomon's had three.

The Late Bronze Age temple at Hazor (area H) has also been mentioned as a prototype for the Jerusalem temple.[47] This is, however, incorrect. The Hazor temple was originally (MB IIC) a one-room temple of the broad-room type with an entrance hall each side of which was "flanked by two rooms (or towers)."[48] In the Late Bronze period it was extended and so became a

---

[39] Cf. Y. Aharoni, *The Land of the Bible,* p. 53, and map. 3 on p. 40.

[40] Cf. M. Ottosson, *Gilead,* p. 217.

[41] Cf. Kenneth H. Waters, *Herodotus on Tyrants and Despots. A Study in Objectivity* (Historia. Zeitschrift für die alte Geschichte, Einzelschriften, Heft 15), Wiesbaden 1971, p. 97.

[42] See the summary of the discussion in Th. A. Busink, *Der Tempel von Jerusalem* I, pp. 558ff., and 582ff. It should be noted that no Phoenician temple from the 10th century B.C. has been found.

[43] D. Ussishkin, "King Solomon's Palaces," *BA* 36/73, pp. 87ff.

[44] For the report, see C.W. McEvan, "The Syrian Expedition of the Oriental Institute of The University of Chicago," *AJA* 41/37, pp. 8f.

[45] A.G. Barrois, *Manuel d'archéologie biblique* II, 1953, p. 443, cf. A. Kuschke, "Der Tempel Salomos und der 'syrische Tempeltypus'," *BZAW* 105, Berlin 1967, pp. 124ff.

[46] Cf. Th. A. Busink, *op. cit.,* pp. 561f.

[47] Y. Yadin, *Hazor. The Head of All Those Kingdoms, Joshua 11:10,* London 1972, p. 86.

[48] *Op. cit.,* p. 76.

three-room temple. One should note that the middle room at Hazor was the smallest one. In Solomon's temple the middle room was the largest and was of the long-room cella type.[49]

M. Ottosson recently advocated that the plans of Solomon's temple and palaces had Egyptian prototypes.[50] He stated that Amarna architecture was introduced into Palestine in connection with houses as well as temples. For the latter he refers to the temples of Beth-Shan. If, however, the Amarna style influenced the architecture at Beth-Shan, it was certainly not the Aton temple whose layout differed from the two temples of strata VII and VI as well as that of stratum IX. Ottosson, following A. Rowe,[51] viewed all of them as representatives of the Amarna style particularly those built close to the palace.[52] However, from Tell el-Amarna we know only that "some small chapels" were built in the same style as the above mentioned Beth-Shan temples.[53] Moreover, the finds from these Beth-Shan temples cannot be characterized as products of the art of the Amarna period.[54] The layout of the temples of strata VII and VI at Beth-Shan has a north-south orientation which was not uncommon for Canaanite temples of the Late Bronze Age,[55] cf. the Hazor temple of area H. The temple of stratum VI is from post-Amarna time.[56] This means that if the city of Beth-Shan was an Egyptian garrison city at that time, it is doubtful that so-called Egyptian buildings were built in the Amarna style since that type of architecture ended with Amarna itself.[57] If Solomon's inspiration did indeed come from Egypt, it

---

[49] Cf. my critique in "Heaven on Earth – at Hazor and Arad," *Religious Syncretism in Antiquity,* ed. by B.A. Pearson, Missoula, Mont. 1975, p. 71, n. 1. Even if there is no Canaanite prototype for Solomon's temple, it seems to be evident that the long-room cella was common in Canaan, cf. Th.A. Busink, *op. cit.,* p. 592.

[50] "Tempel och Palats i Jerusalem och Beth Shan," *SEÅ* 41-42/76-77, pp. 166f., cf. now Ottosson, *Temples and Cult Places in Palestine* (Boreas 12), Uppsala 1980, pp. 113, 118.

[51] *The Four Canaanite Temples of Beth Shan I,* Philadelphia 1940, pp. 3 *et passim,* Ottosson, *op. cit.,* pp. 165ff.

[52] Ottosson considers the "Southern temple" to be a palace built close to the "Northern temple," *Temples and Cult Places,* p. 113. The above mentioned acropolis phenomenon may show that there is nothing specifically Egyptian in building palace and temple close to each other.

[53] R. Giveon, *The Impact of Egypt on Canaan* (Orbis Biblicus et Orientalis 20), Freiburg und Göttingen 1978, p. 25.

[54] Giveon, p. 24f.

[55] Cf. A. Kempinski, "Beth Shan," *Encyclopedia of Archaeological Excavations in the Holy Land* I, Jerusalem 1975, p. 214.

[56] Kempinski, *op. cit.,* p. 214, R. Giveon, *op. cit.,* p. 25.

[57] It is not enough to refer to houses in Amarna only. For a comparison it is necessary to determine whether there was a special "Amarna house (or temple) type" in Egypt during the Amarna age, a type that then was spread by Egyptian officials to the dominions.

was not from Amarna, but may have been from some other place like Thebes or Tanis.[58]

Although there are indications of foreign influence on the Jerusalem temple, it is also possible that Solomon's architects (or the king himself) created a temple, the exact parallel of which has not yet been found.[59] Consequently, Solomon's temple may be an Israelite contribution to the architecture of the ancient Near East.[60]

From what has been said above about kings as city builders, Solomon's large-scale construction endeavors can be put into perspective. His kingdom was very young and was composed of diverse elements, both Israelite and Canaanite (included in the term "Canaanite" are all non-Israelites[61]). The biblical texts state that Solomon rebuilt and fortified the cities of Gezer, Hazor, Lower Beth-Horon, Baalath and Tamar[62] among others, in addition to building store-cities[63] and cities for his chariots and horses (mares),[64]

---

[58] F. Wachtsmuth has pointed to the fact that many Egyptian temples had "Langräume" and "Langhallen" with pillars, cf. those at Luxor and Medinet Habu. Therefore, a comparison between Solomon's temple and Egyptian architecture would be more legitimate than a comparison with Assyrian buildings. However, he thinks that such phenomena as longrooms etc., could independently have come into existence in Jerusalem, *Der Raum* I, Marburg 1929, p. 96f.

[59] Cf. Th. A. Busink, *Der Tempel von Jerusalem* I, p. 617.

[60] For the different types of Syro-Palestinian temples, see also D. Ussishkin, "Building IV in Hamath and the Temples of Solomon and Tell Tayanat," *IEJ* 16/66, pp. 104ff., cf. pp. 174ff., A. Kuschke, "Temple," *Biblisches Reallexikon*, ed. by K. Galling, Tübingen 1977, pp. 333ff. Kuschke maintains that a type that is close to the Solomonic temple type is the "Antentempel" at Tell Chüera, *BZAW* 105, 1967, p. 132. It should be added that R. de Vaux considered Adoram, whom he believed was a Phoenician, to be the architect of the temple in Jerusalem, *Ancient Israel* II, New York and Toronto (1961), 1965, p. 318.

[61] The biblical writer of I Kings 9:21 mentions the Amorites, the Hittites, the Perezzites, the Hivites and the Jebusites, and he states that these were made "forced levy of slaves, and so they are until this day." This may be an overstatement. From the viewpoint of the late Judean writer who, in principle, disliked foreigners, no Israelite would be made a slave. They were, instead, soldiers and commanders of the chariots and horses, v. 22. However, in 5:27, it is said that Solomon's levy was made out of "all Israel", which may be more realistic. It certainly would concern all groups of people within the country. Mettinger sees this as referring to the northern people, which partly explains the split of the Solomonic kingdom, *Solomonic State Officials*, p. 136. Cf. also A.F. Rainey, "Compulsory Labor Gangs in Ancient Israel," *IEJ* 20/70, p. 202, E. Nielsen, *Shechem*, p. 205.

[62] According to S. Mittmann, Tamar is identical with עִיר הַתְּמָרִים, the city of palm trees, in Dt. 34:3, "Ri i, 16f und das Siedlungsgebiet der kenitischen Sippe Hobab," *ZDPV* 93/77, pp. 220ff.

[63] The "store-cities," ערי המשכנות, are, according to J. Gray, probably Solomon's provincial capitals, "the seats of the fiscal officers listed in ch. 4," *I & II Kings*, p. 249. The Hebrew phrase should be compared with the Akkad, *maškanum* (v. Soden: "Stelle der Hinlegens", *maškantum/maškattum*, "Depot").

[64] See D.R. Ap-Thomas, "All the King's Horses," *Proclamation and Presence*, ed.

1 Kings 9:15-19, 10:28, cf. 2 Chr. 8:44f. The fortified cities were not rebuilt solely for military purposes. Strongholds were components of the administrative system[65] and, as such, part of their population was composed of civil servants, including priests. This practice may be a continuation of the Late Bronze Age administrative system.

The textual material reveals that Solomon's building program was primarily carried out in non-Judean areas, such as in the Galilee, the Jezreel valley, the mountains of Ephraim and in the Negeb. The king's policy was, of course, to bind the different areas together. Through these building activities, the arm of the central administration was extended throughout the country making the different groups of people aware that they were united.[66] Military personnel and such civil servants as priests, were a daily reminder of this fact.[67]

That the tenth century B.C. was a time of consolidation of the Israelite kingdom is testified to by the great building activities of Solomon. In addition to textual information, there is archaeological evidence from places not mentioned in the Old Testament. For instance, at Tell Qasīle, stratum IX, the remains of a casemate wall and what has been labelled a public building were uncovered. According to the excavator this stratum represents the first Israelite settlement.[68] However, that depends upon how one defines the word 'Israelite'. On the one hand, if it means that a new population, Israelite, settled in the town, more proof is needed. If, on the other, it means that the city entered the sphere of Israelite dominance, then the population may have remained non-Israelite, adding only officials of the new government. This seems to be the conclusion of A. Mazar who maintains that "the population did not change to any serious extent and that the local traditions

---

by J.I. Durham & J.R. Porter, Richmond, Virginia, 1970, pp. 135-151. These strongholds needed experienced commanders and they were probably not all of Israelite descent, cf. J. Gray, *op. cit.*, p. 252.

[65] Cf. K.-H. Bernhardt, in *Beiträge zur sozialen Struktur des alten Vorderasien*, Berlin 1971, pp. 145f. It should be noted that Solomon rebuilt and fortified cities in areas which, of course, had not been Israelite before the monarchy, cf. A. Alt, "The Formation of the Israelite State in Palestine," *Essays in Old Testament History and Religion*, Garden City, N.Y., 1967, p. 293. He also is said to have built store-cities in Hamath and on Lebanon, I Kings 9:19, 2 Chr. 8:3f.

[66] It is this forced unity that the biblical writers used as an ideal when writing their history of the Israelite and Judahite peoples. Here de Geus' opinion about the tribes should be considered. He maintains that the "system of tribes was created to form an artificial framework connecting groups that formerly were politically fairly independent of each other," *The Tribes of Israel*, p. 118. For "die gross-israelitische Idee," see K. Galling, *Die Erwählungstraditionen Israels* (BZAW 38), Giessen 1928, pp. 68ff.

[67] For the Israelite and Judean kings building sanctuaries and appointing priests in the cities of their kingdoms, cf. 2 Kings 23:5, 19.

[68] B. Maisler, "Excavations at Tell Qasîle, *IEJ* 1/50-51, pp. 136ff., 200.

were kept."[69] From a religious point of view this had certain consequences. That the temple from stratum X was rebuilt in stratum IX may indicate that the cult continued as before. Accordingly, the Israelite officials and merchants who settled in the city also worshipped at this temple in conformance with the law, *mišpāṭ*, of religion in that part of the world. One worshipped the gods of the place. Moreover, it is probable that a priest was sent out from Jerusalem to "teach" the people the religion of the new nation. As a result, Yahwistic rituals were integrated into the temple practice.

Remains of fortresses were also excavated at Tell Arad,[70] Ḥorvat Ritma,[71] Beer-Sheba,[72] Tel 'Amal,[73] and 'En Gev. At the latter, located ca. 5 km from the eastern shore of Lake Tiberias, a citadel with a casemate wall ascribed to the time of Solomon was found.[74] Tell ed-Duweir should also be mentioned since excavations there have revealed a sanctuary from the tenth century B.C.[75] From Trans-Jordan excavations at Tell er-Rumeith unearthed a small citadel "with the east fort wall under 40 meters long." In its earliest period, stratum VIII (10th c. B.C.), "its dimensions were roughly 37 by 32 m."[76] This place has (tentatively) been identified with Ramoth-Gilead[77] which is listed as one of the "Levitical cities" in Josh. 21:38,[78] and as the seat of one of Solomon's governors, ben Geber, in 1 Kings 4:13.[79] If this information is reliable, it may be posited that Levites were stationed there as government officials.[80] Because no remains from the time before the 10th century were found at Tell er-Rumeith, if the above mentioned identification is correct, it means that the passage in Josh. 21 cannot refer to a time before the united monarchy.

In the new kingdom of David and Solomon the security of the highways and of the trade routes through the more sparsely populated areas was of paramount importance. Solomon took special interest in the south through

---

[69] "Excavations at Tell Qasîle, 1973–1974," *IEJ* 25/75, p. 88.

[70] See below.

[71] Z. Meshel, "Ḥorvat Ritma – An Iron Age Fortress in the Negev Highlands," *Tel Aviv* 4/77, pp. 110-135.

[72] Cf. below.

[73] S. Levy and G. Edelstein, "Cinq années de fouilles à Tell 'Amal (Nir David)," *RB* 79/72, pp. 325-367.

[74] B. Mazar –A. Biran –M. Dotan –I. Dunayevsky, *IEJ* 14/64, pp. 1ff.

[75] Y. Aharoni, "Trial Excavation in the 'Solar Shrine' at Lachish," *IEJ* 18/68, pp. 157ff., "Lachish," *IEJ* 18/68, p. 255, and "The Solomonic Temple, The Tabernacle and the Arad Sanctuary," *Orient and Occident* (AOAT 22), 1973, p. 6, *Investigations at Lachish. The Sanctuary and the Residency* (Lachish V), Tel Aviv 1975, pp. 3-11.

[76] P.W. Lapp, *The Tale of the Tell,* ed. by Nancy Lapp, Pittsburgh 1975, pp. 113f.

[77] N. Glueck, *Explorations in Eastern Palestine* (AASOR 25-28), Cambridge, Mass. 1951, pp. 98ff., P.W. Lapp, *RB* 70/63, pp. 406ff., and *RB* 75/68, pp. 98ff.

[78] Cf. 1 Chr. 6:80.

[79] Cf. M. Ottosson, *Gilead*, p. 220.   [80] See further below, pp. 47ff.

which he had access to the Gulf of Aqaba. The Gulf and the Red Sea became one of his main arteries of trade, cf. 1 Kings 9:26.[81] In order to secure the trade from the Gulf of Aqaba to Jerusalem and other places in his kingdom, it was necessary to build "a network of fortresses" along the routes.[82] The fortress and its temple at Arad may be one example of this policy.[83] It is possible that such constructions led to a population increase in the Negeb, a geographical area which, by the way, saw an increase in settlements in the Early Iron I period.[84]

This does not mean that one can jump to the conclusion that all these new settlements were Israelite, as does Y. Aharoni.[85] Nor can one conclude that some of the settlements, such as that of Tel Masos, were built by Israelite seminomads, as does A. Kempinski.[86] The latter maintains that both the settlers of Tel Masos and those of Tel Ṣippor (in the Shephelah) were "well integrated into the culture of their Canaanite neighbors.[87] Indeed, from this, the conclusion that Canaanites from the Shephelah moved to the Negeb can be drawn just as well.[88] They may have moved there for the same reasons that others withdrew to the hill country.[89]

---

[81] S. Yeivin sees in Solomon's maritime expeditions a joint Tyrian-Israelite "initiative to break the Egyptian monopoly" of the lucrative Red Sea trade, "Did the Kingdoms of Israel have a Maritime Policy?" *JQR* 50/59-60, pp. 199f.

[82] M. Evenari–L. Shanan–N. Tadmor, *The Negev. The Challenge of a Desert*, Cambridge, Mass., 1971, p. 17, cf. also Y. Aharoni, "Forerunners of the Limes: Iron Age Fortresses in the Negev," *IEJ* 17/16, pp. 1ff.

[84] Several small fortresses have been found in the central Negeb north of Kadesh-Barnea. Aharoni thinks that some of these were built before the time of the monarchy, "Tel Beer-Sheba, 1975," *IEJ* 25/75, p. 170, cf. "Nothing Early and Nothing Late: Rewriting Israel's Conquest," *BA* 39/76, pp. 55ff. Concerning the settlement problems in the area, see S. Mittmann, "Ri. 1, 16f. und das Siedlungsgebiet der kenitischen Sippe Hobab," *ZDPV* 93/77, pp. 213-35.

[85] *IEJ* 25/75, p. 170, cf. *BA* 39/76, p. 60.

[86] In A. Kempinski–V. Fritz, "Excavations at Tel Masos (Khirbet el-Meshâsh). Preliminary Report of the Third Season, 1975," *Tel Aviv* 4/77, p. 144.

[87] *Op. cit.*, p. 144. Kempinski emphasizes that the pottery types show "close affinities with the late 13th century pottery of the Shephelah. It is not yet possible to determine which types should be regarded as 'Israelite' and which were borrowed from the Canaanite potters," p. 146. If that is the case, how can one be so certain that the settlers were Israelites? What Kempinski is saying is that the material culture is that of the Canaanites. First with David did this area come under the Israelite crown.

[88] It should be remembered that different ethnic groups like the Kenites, Jerahmelites, Calebites, Amalekites and other Edomites settled this area and part of what later became southern Judah. Part of the district south of the Judean highlands was the area in which David carried out his plundering campaigns during his "Philistine" period, I Sam. 27:8ff. One could thus view the destruction of some of the Negeb settlements (around 1000 B.C.) as the result of David's raids. – Concerning the Simeonites, it should be added that S. Mittmann maintains that "ein simeonitisches Siedlungsgebiet hat es im Negeb niemals gegeben," *ZDPV* 93/77, p. 218.

[89] Cf. Ahlström, *JNES* 39/80, pp. 65f.

The fortress of Arad in the Negeb provides an excellent example of the relationship between royal administration and national religion. It is possible that this fortress was placed in an area that had recently been claimed by the Israelite government (by David). Its location is on the so-called "way to Edom", cf. 2 Kings 3:20, which connects the Beer-Sheba-Hebron-Jerusalem highway with the Arabah and the Gulf of Aqaba. The fortress evidences the royal policy of protecting the area and, in particular, this trade route.[90] The building of the fortress has been attributed to Solomon (stratum XI).[91] A temple was included in the complex and represents the official state cult. Priests and the military were the extended arms of the government, the reins by which the king kept his subjects within the law. A temple included as part of a fortress can perhaps be labelled a בית ממלכה, "a temple of the kingdom,"[92] a phrase which occurs in Amos 7:13. The Arad temple cannot be called a border-temple because its location was at least 40 km (ca. 25 miles) away from the nearest border.

B. Mazar advocated that the Arad temple was the successor of a Kenite cultplace taken over by the invading Israelites who built the temple but let the Kenites continue as priests serving the Israelites.[95] The basis for his discussion is that the excavators found "a small open---village" with a cult place (stratum XII). This settlement has been dated to the 11th century B.C. and both Y. Aharoni[94] and B. Mazar[95] identified its settlers as Kenites, cf. Judges 1:16. However, their hypothesis is unrealistic since it is more probable that a king would appoint his own men (representing the Jerusalem line) as priests in a royal temple rather than use personnel from the local population. It should be added that Arad was not a city. It was a fortress compound and its small area, 50 × 50 m.[96] could accommodate few more than government employees.

The many ostraca and seals (of a later time) found within its walls also

---

[90] For a short report about the excavation and its finds, see Y. Aharoni, "Arad: Its Inscriptions and Temple," *BA* 31/68, pp. 2ff., and "The Negev," in *Archaeology and the Old Testament Study*, ed. by D. Winton Thomas, Oxford 1967, pp. 392ff. Because no detailed excavation report has been published, it is impossible to discuss the stratification of the datings given by Aharoni.

[91] For a somewhat later dating of the temple, see Y. Yadin, "A Note on the Stratigraphy of Arad," *IEJ* 15/65, p. 180.

[92] Concerning the term ממלכה being used about kings or royalty, see, for instance, W.L. Moran, "A Kingdom of Priests," *The Bible in Current Catholic Thought*, ed. by J.L. McKenzie, 1962, pp. 15ff., M. Dahood, "Hebrew-Ugaritic Lexicography V," *Biblica* 48/67, p. 426, A. Cody, "When is the Chosen People called a gŏy," *VT* 14/64, p. 3.

[93] "The Sanctuary of Arad and the Family of Hobab the Kenite," *JNES* 24/65, pp. 297ff. G. Boling follows Mazar and assumes that Arad was used "only as a seasonal (Qenite?) high place," *Judges* (Anchor Bible 6A), Garden City, N.Y., 1975, pp. 57f.

[94] *BA* 31/68, p. 4.

[95] *Op. cit.,* pp. 302ff.

[96] The temple area is 20 × 15 m.

indicate Arad's status as a government compound. Some of the ostraca give orders to the commanding officer of the fortress.[97] The opening formulae of these writings have been seen as echoing those of the Amarna letters.[98] That the style of administrative writing in Palestine was influenced by the Egyptian tradition is highly probable if one takes into consideration the fact that Egypt politically dominated Palestine from the 18th Dynasty[99] down to the beginning of the Iron Age.[100]

The occurrence of personal names found on the ostraca supports the opinion that Arad was not only part of the royal administration as a military base but was also an arm of the national cultic establishment. Among the names are Meremoth (Arad no. 50) and Pashur (no. 54), and the phrase the "sons of Qoraḥ" (no. 49).[101] One of the ostraca, addressed to the commander Elyashib, mentions the Qerosite (no. 18). According to Ezra 2:44 and Neh. 7:47, the family of Qeros belonged to a class of temple servants (the נתינים). Consequently, it is possible that this ostracon reveals their existence as a class of cultic employees in pre-exilic time.[102] Moreover, the name of the commandant (or chief administrator), Elyashib, is of certain interest. The name is known in the Old Testament from priestly circles, cf. 1 Chr. 24:12, Neh. 3:1, 20f., 12:10,22f., 13:4, 28. Therefore, it is not improbable that he had Levitical ancestry.[103]

---

97 Y. Aharoni, "Seals and Royal Functionaries from Arad," *Eretz Israel* 8/67, pp. 101ff. (Hebrew), *Arad Inscriptions* (Judean Desert Series), Jerusalem 1975, cf. also D. Pardee, "Letters from Tel Arad," *UF* 10/78, pp. 289-336, A. Lemaire, *Inscriptions hébraiques,* Paris 1977, pp. 145-235.

98 Aharoni, *BA* 38/61, p. 13. For the types of introductory formulae, see also M. Weippert, "Zum Präskript der hebräischen Briefe von Arad," *VT* 25/75, pp. 202-212. Weippert also draws attention to parallels with Phoenician and Aramaic (Elephantino) toxto. Conoult aloo D. Pardoo, "An Ovorviow of Anoiont Hobrow Epiotolography," *JBL* 97/78, pp. 321ff.

99 Cf. E.W. Heaton, *Solomon's New Men. The Emergence of Ancient Israel as a Nation,* New York 1974, pp. 12f.

100 It should be added that Egyptian hieratic numerals were used in Palestine both in the Late Bronze period as well as in the Iron Age period, Y. Aharoni, "The Use of Hieratic Numerals in Hebrew Ostraca and the Shekel Weights," *BASOR* 184/66, p. 19, W.H. Shea, "The Inscribed Late Bronze Jar Handle from Tell Ḥalif," *BASOR* 232/78, pp. 78ff.

101 Aharoni, *BA* 31/68, pp. 10ff. For the term *qrḥ* as referring to an "acropolis", see above, p. 16. Concerning the phrase *bĕnē qōraḥ* one could ask whether it has anything to do with being baldheaded or whether it implies a certain temple place. From the cultic laws we know that the priests were not permitted to shave off their hair, Lev. 21:5, Ezek 44:20, cf. Dt. 14:1. For Pashur as an Egyptian name, see M. Noth, *Die israelitischen Personennamen im Rahmen der gemeinsemitischen Namengebung.* Stuttgart 1928, p. 63.

102 See the discussion by B.A. Levine, "Notes on a Hebrew Ostracon from Arad," *IEJ* 19/69, pp. 49-51. The ostraca with the name Elyashib are, according to Aharoni, from 598/97 B.C., *IEJ* 16/66, pp. 1-7.

103 It should be added that the "Kittim" mentioned in some of the ostraca from

Another place to be considered in this connection is the city of Beer-Sheba in southern Judah. No building remains from the Bronze Age have been found on the tell,[104] and the first fortified city is dated to the 10th century B.C. Because of the planning of the city, Y. Aharoni concluded that it was not only a royal citadel but was also a district capital.[105] Thus, Beer-Sheba too, is an example of the great building activity of the new nation that rose to power in Canaan ca. 1000 B.C. Its location in the southern part of Judah, north of the Sinai desert, may have made it an important military base. If that is true, its cultic establishment was part of the Jerusalem-centered national religion. From the textual material we know that the city was a famous pilgrimage place, cf. Am. 5:5, 8:14. Therefore, it is possible that it had more than one cult place and that the large horned altar, found inside the city not far from the city gate, belonged not only to the official Yahweh cult place, but to another cult place as well. The exact location of the sanctuary to which this altar belonged is not yet known.[106]

Recently, another Judean fortress was found, namely, Kuntillet 'Ajrud, located in the northern Sinai ca. 50 km. south of Kadesh-Barnea on a hill close to the highway Darb el-Ghazze, "the way of Gaza." [107] Even if it is from a later time, it demonstrates, as does the Arad fortress, the intimate

---

Arad can be understood as Greek mercenaries in the service of the Judean king, as was probably also the case with the Kittim at the fortress of Meṣad Hashavyahu on the coast and at Tell Milḥ south of Arad, Aharoni, *BA* 31/68, pp. 13f., and H. Tadmor, "Philistia under Assyrian Rule," *BA* 29/66, p. 102, n. 59. S. Yeivin sees in the Kittim an indication that Arad was not a Yahwistic sanctuary, "On the Use and Misuse of Archaeology in Interpreting the Bible," *American Academy for Jewish Research, Proceedings* 34/66, pp. 152ff. The mention of the "sons of Qoraḥ" and the above mentioned priest names may contradict Yeivin. Whether the Kittim were stationed at Arad or not is impossible to decide, cf. Y. Yadin, "Four Epigraphical Queries," *IEJ* 24/74, pp. 30ff. Ostracon no. 4 may indicate that the Kittim were stationed in the vicinity.

[104] Sherds from the Chalcolithic period and from the 12th and 11th centuries B.C. provide some interesting hints about the settlement history of the tell, see Y. Aharoni, *Beer-Sheba I. Excavations at Tel Beer-Sheba* (Tel Aviv Institute of Archaeology, Publications 2), Tel Aviv 1973, p. 4.

[105] *Op. cit.*, pp. 17, 110.

[106] Aharoni, "The Horned Altar of Beer-Sheba," *BA* 37/74, pp. 2ff., and "Tel Beersheba," *IEJ* 24/74, pp. 271ff., Y. Yadin, "Beer-sheba: The High Place Destroyed by King Josiah," *BASOR* 222/76, pp. 5ff. Yadin maintains that the builders of bāmôth (he associates the altar with a bāmāh, a term he does not define) "were not guided" by the prohibitions in the Mosaic law and, therefore, the *bāmôt*-cult was dedicated to foreign gods, p. 11. Yadin did not substantiate this accusation. The Mosaic law may not have been in existence at that time. Indeed, it seems to be a law for the reconstruction of post-exilic society. For a critique of Yadin's theories about the location of the sanctuary of Beer-Sheba, see Z. Herzog–A.F. Rainey–Sh. Moshkovitz, "The Stratigraphy at Beer-sheba and the Location of the Sanctuary," *BASOR* 225/77, pp. 49-58. It should be added that from what is being maintained in this investigation, the term *bāmôt* often refers to royal Israelite and Judahite sanctuaries, see pp. 46, 59f.

[107] Z. Meshel and C. Meyer, "The Name of God in the Wilderness of Zin," *BA* 39/

relationship between military defense and national religion. The pottery found here suggests that the buildings are from the 9th–8th centuries B.C. One of the rooms inside the entrance of the western building has been characterized as a bench-room "where people deposited their offerings."[108] This room could, therefore, be seen as the cult room of the fortress. Among the finds, the stone vessels and wall plaster with inscriptions should be mentioned.[109] There are also some pithoi with drawings of deities (i.e. the Egyptian Bes). One of these has an inscription with the phrase *brktk lyhwh... wl'šrth*, "may you be blessed to Yahweh... and to his Asherah."[110] This shows that Yahweh had a consort, a *paredros*, at his side, namely, Asherah.[111] The importance of this is threefold. It is one more example of the fact that the royal establishment was expressed in military and religious forms. It also gives us rare information about the extension of the Judean kingdom of that time, and it illustrates the dimensions of the official Judean religion. It can be concluded that this find corrects the picture of the religious history of Judah as advocated by the later biblical writers. Their censorship has been broken.[112]

76, pp. 6ff. For some reason the authors do not mention the Asherah phenomenon in this report.

[108] Z. Meshel, "Did Yahweh have a Consort? The New Religious Inscriptions from the Sinai," *Biblical Archaeology Review* 5/79, pp. 24ff.

[109] A so called cult room (room no. 49) also with benches has been found at Tell ed-Duweir, see Y. Aharoni, *Investigations at Lachish. The Sanctuary and the Residency (Lachish V)*, Tel Aviv 1975, pp. 26ff.

[110] Meshel, *op. cit.*, pp. 31f.

[111] Through an earlier literary analysis, I arrived at the same conclusions, see my book *Aspects of Syncretism in Israelite Religion*, pp. 50ff.

[112] That Yahweh had a consort, Meshel considers "a thoroughly blasphemous notion," *op. cit.*, p. 31. Yet, how can the official Judean religion be called blasphemous? Because the pottery and the script are said to show Phoenician influences Meshel draws the hasty conclusion that the mentioning of gods "other than Jehovah"(!) most probably points to the time of Queen Athaliah of Judah, "Kuntillet 'Ajrud. An Israelite Religious Center in Northern Sinai", *Expedition* 20:4, 1978, pp. 50-54. One could object to this by saying that even if the script is Phoenician in style (which is not that much different from what could be called south Palestinian, cf. also, for instance, the Mesha inscription) it does not mean that the religious establishment of Judah had more Phoenician influences at this place than the official religion of the kingdom had had since the days of David and Solomon. The Judahites do not need to be excused because an inscription from Kuntillet 'Ajrud informs us about their state religion. Indeed they had long worshipped Asherah. To return to the "Phoenician style" of the inscriptions it is hard to discuss this before a complete edition of the text (with plates) has been published. From Meshel's (p. 33) published photo it seems doubtful that the inscriptions are purely Phoenician in style. For instance, the *dalet* is that of the 9th–8th century *dalet* of Hebrew seals. On Phoenician seals this form does not occur. The *kap* is also closer to that of the Hebrew seals of the same time, as is the *lamed*. The *bet* and the *nun* seem to be 8th century Hebrew forms. Consult L.G. Herr, *The Scripts of Ancient Northwest Semitic Seals*, Missoula, Mont., 1978.

CHAPTER FOUR

ROYAL PRIESTHOOD

Exactly how Solomon's district organization affected the cultic establishment and its priesthood is not known. However, since military and civil administrative posts were increased, it may be assumed that posts for religious personnel also multiplied. (This is applicable if civil and cultic personnel were two distinct groups which was not always the case.) Although the textual material does not disclose whether there was a government sanctuary in every district capital, if the close ties between administration, military and cult are taken into account, it is very likely. Presumably, taxes and tithes that were consigned the sacral sphere were stored in a special place — a sanctuary, chapel, or "cult room" — in the government complex.[1] If the districts were divided into smaller areas, each having its own subcenter, then there were many such places to deposit taxes and sacrificial gifts.[2]

Districts capitals like Ramoth-Gilead,[3] Ta'anak,[4] Beth-Shan,[5] probably Mahanaim (Eshba'al's capital), and Shechem appear to have had a cult place.[6] Beth-Shemesh may be added to these, especially since its name refers to a site well-known for its sun worship. Because nothing indicates that this cult ceased when the city became part of the Israelite kingdom, it may be assumed that rituals dedicated to Yahweh were incorporated into it.

Among other district capitals, Dor is worth mentioning. A seal found near Samaria-Sebastiye had led to speculation about whether Yahweh was worshipped there.[7] According to N. Avigad's reconstruction the seal bears

---

[1] Cf. Am. 4:4.

[2] E. Stern identified the house found at Tel Mevorakh (stratum VIII, tenth century B.C.) as an administrative building of one of the sub-districts of Dor, *Excavations at Tel Mevorakh 1973–1976. Part One: From the Iron Age to the Roman Period* (Qedem 9), Jerusalem 1978, p. 77.

[3] According to G.E. Wright, Ramoth-Gilead "was founded by Solomon to be the district administrative center," "The Provinces of Solomon," *Eretz Israel* 8/67, p. 67*.

[4] For the "cultic structure" (tenth century B.C.) at Ta'anak, see P.W. Lapp, "The 1963 Excavations at Ta'annek", *BASOR* 173/64, pp. 26ff., *The Tale of the Tell*, p. 95.

[5] The buildings of stratum V (cf. 1 Sam. 31:10, 1 Chr. 10:10) may have been in use during the time of Solomon. F.W. James dates the lower stratum V to the period ca. 1100–900 B.C., *The Iron Age at Beth-Shan*, Philadelphia 1966, pp. 30ff., 140ff.

[6] G.E. Wright, *Encyclopaedia of Archaeological Excavations in the Holy Land* IV, Jerusalem 1978, p. 1093.

[7] M. Haran, "A Temple at Dor," *IEJ* 27/77, pp. 12-15.

the inscription ‏[לז]‏ ‏כריו כהן דאר‏ , "[belonging to Ze]charyahu, priest of Dor."[8] Even if this seal is dated to the mid-eighth century B.C., it may still indicate that Dor long had a sanctuary since it seems to have been one of the very old cities (city-states) of Canaan. Its existence is attested by the recently found tablets from Tell Mardikh (ancient Ebla)[9] in Syria which are dated to about the 24th century B.C. From the Amarna tablets we know that Dor was under Egyptian administration.[10] According to the Wen-Amun report, at the time of the raids of the Sea-peoples, Dor and its surroundings were populated by the *ṭkr*.[11] In the Old Testament Dor is mentioned as a participant in a Canaanite coalition against the Israelites at the battle of Meron, Josh. 11:2. In Josh. 12:23 the king of Nephat-Dor is listed as one of the defeated Canaanite kings. This indicates that the biblical writer did not distinguish between the Tjeker and the Canaanites; all enemies were labelled Canaanites. According to Judg. 1:27 the "tribe" of Manasseh was unable to conquer Dor, Beth-Shan, Ta'anak, Ibleam, and Megiddo. This means that those areas later considered to be the Manasseh territory were not so during the pre-monarchic period. Moreover, it indicates that the city-state Nephat-Dor[12] was incorporated into the Israelite nation under David, if not later. According to V. Fritz, Josh. 12:9-24 contains a list of cities (some of which did not exist in the Early Iron Age I) all of which were fortified by Solomon. Because this list includes Dor, Fritz maintains that it became Israelite during Solomon's reign (Iron IIA).[13] Be that as it may, when Dor, an important

---

[8] "The Priest of Dor," *IEJ* 25/75, pp. 101ff. The seal has the Egyptian uraeus which was a divine and royal symbol. This, again, shows the Egyptian cultural influence in Palestine. Here one should also note Avigad's statement that "priesthood in Israel was royal appointment," p. 104.

[9] Cf. G. Pettinato, "The Royal Archives of Tell Mardikh-Ebla," *BA* 39/76, p. 46, cf. *Orientalia* 44/75, pp. 361ff. For the reading Ibla, see I.J. Gelb, "Thoughts about Ibla: A Preliminary Evaluation, March 1977," *Syro-Mesopotamian Studies* 1/77, p. 5.

[10] J.A. Knudtzon, *Die El-Amarna Tafeln mit Einleitung und Erläuterungen* (VAB 2:1-2), Leipzig 1915, p. 289. Cf. A. Alt, "Ägyptische Temple in Palästine und die Landnahme der Philister," *Kleine Schriften* I, München 1953, p. 227, n. 3, and "Zur Geschichte von Beth-Sean," *KS* I, pp. 246ff., S. Herrmann, *A History of Israel in Old Testament Times*, p. 90 W. Helck, *Die Beziehungen*, p. 229f.

[11] J.A. Wilson, in *ANET*, p. 26, H. Goedicke, *The Report of Wenamun*, Baltimore and London 1975. According to Goedicke the *ṭkr* were Semites, p. 182.

[12] For Nephat-Dor as a larger area than the city itself, cf. 1 Kings 4:11. It is possible that the area of this city kingdom extended as far as the Philistine territory. Thus, it was about the same size as the later Assyrian province Du'ru established by Tiglath-Pileser III, cf. A. Alt, *KS* II, pp. 188ff. For ‏נפה‏ as a Sea people's term for "wooded area," see the discussion by M. Ben-Dov," ‏נָפָה‏ – Geographical Term of Possible 'Sea People' Origin," *Tel Aviv* 3/76, pp. 70-73.

[13] "Die sogenannte Liste der besiegten Könige in Jos. 12," *ZDPV* 85/69, pp. 136ff. M. Noth maintained that Solomon only took the "Hinterland" of Dor and not the city itself at the time of his district division, *Könige 1. 1-16* (BK X:1), Neukirchen 1968, p. 70. However, 1 Kings 4:11 seems to contradict this.

port city, became a city or a district capital of Israel, Solomon dispatched
officials (some probably called levites) to let the people of the district know
how to "revere god and king." This does not mean that an Israelite sanctuary
was built in the city. A pre-Israelite sanctuary may have been used as part of
the new government's administrative center. Therefore, we cannot assume,
as does M. Haran, that there was no temple in Dor in which to worship
Yahweh of Israel.[14]

Taking into consideration that kings were temple builders, it is natural to
assume that Solomon's district capitals and his fortresses (cf. Arad) had a
cult place or a cult room which served as the sanctuary of the official state
religion. That sanctuaries were an integral part of the royal administration is
evident from 1 Kings 12:31 and 2 Kings 23:19. According to 1 Kings
12:31, king Jeroboam I built בתי במות, sanctuaries,[15] in his country. From
2 Kings 23:19 we learn that in the Assyrian province of Samerina, king
Josiah of Judah destroyed all the בתי הבמות that the kings of Israel (i.e. the
northern kingdom) had built. Because these sanctuaries were built by the
state and were part of the royal administration, it may be concluded that
they were under the supervision of the district governors. Examples from
Egypt are illustrative. The Egyptian district governors functioned as temple
superintendents ("Tempelkuratoren") at the main temple of the district
capitals.[16] It should be noted that the distinction between priests and other
officials of the crown was not as sharp as has usually been thought. For
example, it was not unknown for a high priest to be appointed vizier.[17] On
the other hand, a Pharaoh might appoint a favorite civil servant to the office
of high priest.[18]

It is possible that such a system was operative in Israel as early as the
time of king Saul. For example, according to 1 Sam. 21:8 (Engl. 21:7),
Saul's servant, עבד, Doeg the Edomite, who was the chief officer over the
shepherds,[19] was נעצר, detached (empowered),[20] for the service of Yahweh

---

[14] *IEJ* 27/77, pp. 12-15. Haran thinks that an Israelite temple had to be built by
David, Solomon, or Jeroboam I, and because the Old Testament does not mention
such a building project, the supposed temple cannot have existed. He also assumes that
the priest of the above mentioned inscription "resided in Dor" but that he held his
cultic service at another place.

[15] For reading plural, see M. Noth, *Könige I. 1-16*, p. 268.

[16] T. Säve-Söderberg, *Ägypten und Nubien*, Lund 1941, p. 68.

[17] E. Otto, *Ägypten. Der Weg des Pharaonenreiches*, 3rd ed., Stuttgart 1958, p. 156.

[18] W.C. Hayes, "Egypt: Internal Affairs from Thutmosis I to the Death of Amenophis III," *CAH* II:1, p. 327. M.F. Gyles, *Pharaonic Policies and Administration, 663 to
323 B.C.* (The James Sprunt Studies in History and Political Science 41), Chapel Hill,
N.C., 1959, gives other examples of the combination of priestly and civil offices, p. 64.

[19] Cf. P.R. Ackroyd, *The First Book of Samuel* (The Cambridge Bible Commentary of the New English Bible), p. 171.

[20] For the root עצר, see E. Kutsch, "Die Wurzel עצר im Hebräischen," *VT* 2/52,

at the temple of Nob. Although we do not know the significance of Doeg's presence at Nob's temple, as the chief officer of the shepherds and their flocks, he may have been acting in a supervisory capacity. If this is correct, the temple of Nob was under the direction of Saul's administration.[21] The same would then have been the case for other sanctuaries.

When David became king in Jerusalem he appointed members of Hebronite "levitical" families as his officials in Transjordan, 1 Chr. 26:30ff.[22] The text states that they were sent out "for all the work of Yahweh and the service of the king." From this one can conclude with R. de Vaux, that the Levites not only officiated as priests but as civil servants, judges and as a "police force" (פקדה) "who supervised all the affairs of Yahweh and the king on both sides of the Jordan."[23] Thus, areas newly incorporated by the king were administered by faithful personnel from his old court and capital, Hebron. Not only did he know and trust these men but they, in turn, probably knew his approach to and system of governance. This was important since the laws of the new government had to be made known and followed, 2 Sam. 8:15,[24] cf. 1 Sam. 10:25.

Another passage should be noted in this connection. In 2 Chr. 17:7ff. king Jehoshaphat of Judah is said to have placed chief officials and Levites in the cities of his kingdom in order to "teach them [the people] the law of Yahweh." This may be the Chronicler's way of referring to the old custom of placing government officials including priests in different cities throughout the nation to instruct the people and to collect taxes, cf. 2 Chr. 24:11.

Priests and Levites were, therefore, part of the government's law enforcement personnel — law here taken in its wider meaning of both civil and religious law, i.e. the "way" of the nation. Consequently, it is natural to suppose that priests and Levites had military and/or guarding duties. The Hebrew word פקדה, which is mentioned in connection with David's placing of Levites in Transjordan, 1 Chr. 26:30ff., and which can be translated "administration", can also mean "guard, class of officers." According to Jer. 29:26 the head priest was the supervisor or commander of the temple guard. In Jer. 20:1-3, the priest Pashur was designated as פקיד נגיד, "chief guards-

---

pp. 57ff., G.W. Ahlström, *BZ* 13/69, pp. 96f., H. Seebass, "Tradition und Interpretation bei Jehu ben Chanani und Ahia von Silo," *VT* 25/75, pp. 182ff.

[21] Thus, Saul was within his rights to punish the priesthood of Nob for supporting an insurgent, David.

[22] This negates M. Haran's thesis that the Levites only "resided" in the "Levitical" cities, "they did not officiate in them." *Temples and Temple-Service in Ancient Israel,* Oxford 1978, pp. 202f. For the problem of the "Levitical" cities, see below.

[23] *Ancient Israel,* New York and Toronto 1965, p. 133.

[24] Cf. the Akkadian phrase *palāḫ ili u šarri,* "to revere, worship, god and king," mentioned above in chapter I in connection with Sargon II's building of Dūr-Sharrukīn, a city which he populated with foreigners who had to be taught the Assyrian way of life. Cf. M. Weinfeld, *Deuteronomy and the Deuteronomic School,* p. 163.

man." The title בעל פקדת, "commander of the guard," occurs in Jer. 37:
13. Ezechiel calls the guardsmen Levites, 44:11, a designation that may be
part of the prophet's "degrading" of the Levites because they had led the
people in idol worship. In connection with the Levites one should also note
the terms צבא and שמר, which, likewise, seem to indicate "military" con-
cerns.[25] These may signify that the Levites were used as a police force to
guard the deity and his sanctuaries, and perhaps also to guard the royal
estates,[26] cf. 1 Chr. 26:30ff. Indeed, it is possible that the men Jehoiadah
(the first priest of the Jerusalem temple) posted at the temple in connection
with the *coup d'état* that culminated in Queen Athaliah's death, constituted
a priestly guard under his command, 2 Kings 11:18.

These examples may reveal an old Syro-Palestinian tradition that is also
found in Anatolia. As mentioned above, a Hittite text, "Instructions for
Temple Officials,"[27] not only states that priests were responsible for guarding the temple but that during the night one of the high-priests was in
charge of the night patrols.[28]

It is possible that Dt. 33:11 reflects the police-force function of priests
and Levites; they were soldiers for god and king. According to this text,
Yahweh is called on to bless the חיל of the Levites and smite "the loins of
his enemies."[29] The term חיל may be translated "army, police force" or
the like. It is, therefore, quite in harmony with an old tradition when
Nehemiah used Levites as "security" guards at the gates of Jerusalem during
the sabbath, Neh. 13:22.

It may be posited that the label "Levite" was a technical term for priests
and government officials stationed at different locations in the kingdom.
This supports a derivation of the word from לוה (*lāwāh*), "to accompany,"
in niph. "to attach oneself to," or "to be bound."[30] These persons were,

---

[25] J. Milgrom, *Studies in Levitical Terminology* I, Berkeley, Cal., 1970, pp. 8ff., cf.
J.R. Spencer, *The Levitical Cities: A Study of the Role and Function of the Levites in
the History of Israel* (Unpubl. Ph.D. diss., University of Chicago), Chicago 1980,
chapter II.

[26] B. Mazar, "The Cities of the Priests and Levites," *SVT* 7, 1960, p. 202.

[27] Cf. above, p. 12, and E.H. Sturtevant and G. Bechtel, *A Hittite Chrestomathy,*
Philadelphia 1935, pp. 127ff., A. Goetze, in *ANET*, pp. 207ff.

[28] Goetze, *ANET*, p. 209. Cf. the discussion by J. Milgrom, *op. cit.,* pp. 50ff.

[29] Concerning the date of Dt. 33, C.H.J. de Geus has maintained that "for lin-
guistic reasons we may not give it a very early date," *The Tribes of Israel,* p. 99.
A. Cody sees the utterance about Levi in verses 9b-10 as stemming from the eighth
century B.C., *A History of Old Testament Priesthood* (Analecta Biblica 35), Rome
1969, p. 120.

[30] Cf., for instance, K. Budde, *Die altisraelitische Religion,* Giessen 1912, p. 137,
E. Dhorme, *L'évolution religieuse d'Israël,* Brussels 1937, p. 227, G. Widengren, "What
do we know about Moses?," *Proclamation and Presence. Old Testament Essays in
Honour of Gwynne Henton Davies,* ed. by J.I. Durham and J.R. Porter, Richmond,
Virg., 1970, pp. 37f., n. 58, cf. also W. von Soden, *Akkadisches Handwörterbuch,*

thus, associated with, or attached, bound, to the central government as its employees. If this is the origin of the social class of Levites, two things must be stressed. In the first place, the Levites never constituted a tribe before the artificial systematization of Yahweh's people into twelve such "tribes." This is supported by the fact that some Levitical families, for instance the Hebronites and the Libnites, came from different goegraphical areas. Moreover, as G. Hölscher maintained, their names are gentilica.[31] Consequently, whether or not the Levites were originally a secular tribe is a moot point. Second, any royal appointee, either in Israel or in Judah, may have been called a Levite. They were not a special clan or priest family during the time of the monarchy. This is supported by the fact that in the biblical texts referring to the premonarchic period Levites are rarely mentioned as priests. In connection with the temple of Dan we learn that its priesthood was "mosaic" and "levitical", Judg. 17-18. The concern of this text was originally to advocate a Yahwistic legitimacy of Dan's priesthood – a legitimacy which must have been questioned, thus, the tradition is rather late. The final commentator has used this to critize the Levites of Dan for worshipping idols, Judg. 18:31,[32] an accusation levelled against them also in Ezek. 44:10.

In times of religious diversity and assimilation such as marked the period of the united Israelite monarchy, it would seem, as a matter of course, that wherever priests/levites served, they were acquainted with idol worship.

---

p. 541. In post-biblical Hebrew that word for "escort" is לְוָיָה . For the stem cf. also the Egyptian place name ra-wi-'i-ri (lawi-ili), "the client of El," J. Simons, Handbook for the Study of Egyptian Topographical Lists Relating to Western Asia, Leiden 1937, p. 165, W. Helck, Die Beziehungen, p. 237, M. Weippert, The Settlement, p. 43, n. 139.

[31] "Levi," Pauly-Wissowa, Real-Encyklopädie der classischen Altertumswissenschaft XII:2, Stuttgart 1924, pp. 2155ff., cf. Aa. Bentzon, Studier over det sadokidiske Praesteskabs Historie, København 1931, p. 59, J. Liver, "Korah, Dathan, and Abiram," Scripta Hierosolymitana 8/61, p. 213, A Cody, A History of the Old Testament Priesthood, p. 161. It is probable that the Mushites belong to the same category. In Nu. 3:17ff. they are connected with the Hebronites and the Libnites, cf. also Nu. 26:58. The association with Moses is, thus, secondary. For a discussion about whether or not the Levites originally constituted a secular tribe, consult J.R. Spencer, op. cit., Chap. II (with lit.). For the Egyptian term rw' referring to southern Palestine, it is impossible to demonstrate that it had anything to do with the Old Testament Levites. Cf. also M. Weippert who maintains that that "the so-called 'secular tribe' of Levi originally had nothing to do with the Levitical priesthood; the two entities were not equated until a considerable time after the disappearance of the tribe from history," The Settlement, p. 43, n. 139.

[32] G.W. Ahlström, Aspects of Syncretism in Israelite Religion, pp. 26f. R.G. Boling sees the text's "complete formation in the amphictyonic period," Judges, p. 266. One should, however, first demonstrate that an amphictyony ever existed before any literature is ascribed to its time. Besides Micha's Levite, another one is mentioned in Judg. 19-20. This Levite was living in Ephraim. Although nothing substantive is known about him, he and his concubine are said to have been the cause of the war between the Benjaminites and the Ephraimites.

Indeed, the prophetic polemic against idols provides a graphic picture of Israelite religion in the pre-exilic period. For example, the above-mentioned passage in Ezek. 44:10f. indicates that not only the Levites but the population they served worshipped Yahweh 'and other gods,[33] in the form of idols, גלולים.[34] From this and from Judg. 17-18 mentioning the Ephraimite petty ruler, Micah, having installed a "Levite" to serve his idol, it may be concluded that the Levites of that time were representatives of a religion that still had no commands against idol worship.

Acknowledging that the Levites were government officials solves the problem of why they were called a "tribe" yet had no "inheritance", נחלה[35] (i.e. a geographical area where they settled), in the land.[36] As officials at national shrines they could not. Their employer, the state or state sanctuary, owned land outside the cities where they lived. In later descriptions of the Levites and their rights this land is called מגרש, "the land which is separated, parcelled off."[37] Viewing the land as part of the payment given to sacral and civil servants it is possible to further elucidate the phenomenon in the light of an Egyptian parallel. In Egypt the priests lived off the fields of the temples. Moreover, these fields were exempt from confiscation.[38] The position of the Levites may have been similar. If too much land had become tax exempt and revenue was needed it is clear why king Josiah's adminis-

---

[33] From the Ezekiel passage one may see the worship of idols being a fact also after the reform of Josiah.

[34] G. Fohrer thinks that the Levites were "more cautious about adopting alien elements than the Jerusalem priests were," *History of Israelite Religion*, transl. by D.E. Green, Nashville and New York 1972, p. 132. Concerning the גלולים, see my *Aspects of Syncretism*, pp. 46ff.

[35] For נחלה as a legal term belonging to the laws of inheritance, cf. J.P. Weinberg, "Die Agrarverhältnisse in der Bürger-Tempel-Gemeinde der Achämenidenzeit," *Acta Antiqua* 22/74, pp. 473ff.

[36] A.H.J. Gunneweg hypothesizes that the Levites were a religious order. They were *gērîm* who had broken off from a tribe and formed their own group, a religious order, dedicated to preserve the amphictyony, *Leviten und Priester* (FRLANT 89), Göttingen 1965, pp. 33ff. For a critique of Gunneweg's hypothesis, see C.H.J. de Geus, *The Tribes of Israel*, p. 98.

[37] This term refers to the area in front of the city wall outside the city and occurs in late texts, Lev. 25:35, Nu. 35:2-7, Josh. 14:4, 21:2-42, Ezek. 27:28, 36:5, 48:15-17, 1 Chr. 5:16, 6:40-66, 13:2, 2 Chr. 11:14, 31:19. The measurements for this kind of land given in Nu. 35:4f. are the same for all cities, and are utopian (1000 cubits [one cubit = 50 cm] 'round about" from the walls of the cities), cf. J. Wellhausen, *Prolegomena*, pp. 159f., M. Haran, *Temples and Temple-Service*, p. 123. L. Delekat translates the word with land "die Stadt als Gürtel umgibt," "Zum hebräischen Wörterbuch," *VT* 14/64, p. 17. For *migrāš* as usufruct for the Levites, see also H. Strauss, *Untersuchungen zu den Überlieferungen der vorexilischen Leviten*, 1960, p. 136.

[38] W. Helck, *Zur Verwaltung des mittleren und neuen Reichs* (Probleme der Ägyptologie 3), Leiden 1958, pp. 120f.

trative reorganization had the potential to become a financial disaster for the Levites.[39]

From the above it is possible to explain why the Levites were "associated" with the category of גרים, "aliens, clients, newcomers."[40] The word *lwy* itself meant a client. As government appointees they were not members of the clans of the district where they lived: they were the clients of the government. Ranking the Levites as a "tribe" is, as already indicated, a construction made to suit the later idea that Israel was composed of twelve "tribes" (the number twelve expressing the ideal of totality). When a history of the two peoples (Israelites and Judahites) was constructed from the Judean viewpoint, all Levites were considered to be descendants of Lewi ben Ya'acob, and all priest classes were given a genealogy linking them to Lewi.[41] In the Judean construction of the "settlement" in Canaan, the Levites were religiously legitimated as the guardians of the Yahweh cult by stating that, upon a command from Yahweh, Moses – the later historiographer's great authority – gave certain cities to the Levites in lieu of part of the country, cf. Nu. 35:1-7, Josh. 14:4, 21:1. Thus was the phenomenon of appointing priests at the national sanctuaries outside the capital remade into an institution and projected back in time. It should be pointed out that it is historically impossible to enact legislation making Canaanite cities part of an Israelite institution long before they were built or became part of the nation Israel. As will be shown below, some of them did not exist before the tenth-ninth centuries B.C. The "institution" is, in all likelihood, a construction.[42] Although its purpose is never mentioned, it may perhaps be seen as an attempt to explain why the Levites as a "tribe" did not have a part of the country as their inheritance.

Levitical cities

A list of "Levitical" cities can be found both in Josh. 21 and in 1 Chr. 6. In the former all these cities are said to have existed during the time of

---

[39] If this was the case, the book of Deuteronomy cannot have been the inspiration for king Josiah's reform. Rather it is a composition after that time.

[40] Cf. Dt. 14:27, 29 which reflect a later time. Nu. 18:21f. mention that the tithes supported the Levites; it is their נחלה, inheritance. Nothing is said about the Levites being priests or sacrificing. Instead we hear that they gave part of the tithe to Aaron. The text, thus, reflects post-exilic time, cf. G. Fohrer, *Introduction to the Old Testament*, p. 143. See also Neh. 10:38 mentioning that a priest has to be with the Levites when they collect the tithe.

[41] For information that a "levitical monopoly" was non-existent in early monarchic time, cf. E. Auerbach, "Der Aufstieg der Priesterschaft zur Macht im Alten Israel," *SVT* 9, 1963, p. 237.

[42] Independently, J.R. Spencer arrived at a similar conclusion, see his concluding chapter in his dissertation *The Levitical Cities*.

Joshua. However, because the author of the "Conquest" theme was concerned about the country, its future and the people of his own time, the
past became very important. In his historiography, the "beginning" was
willed and created by his god, a common Near Eastern feature. In this beginning present knowledge about history and people, etc., played a part and
was projected back into time. In this respect, the purpose of the "Levitical"
cities was to show that they existed before the people came into the light of
history. Of course, the "Levitical" cities could not have come into existence
at the same time as did the people since, according to the historical construction, the land that was promised to Abraham, Gen. 15 and 17:8, had to be
conquered first.[43] The time of the "Conquest" was, thus, a suitable period
for the literal inauguration of the system of the "Levitical" cities.[44] However that may be, if the "Levitical" cities were places where Levites as
government agents were stationed, they could not have come into existence
as an institution before the monarchy. When there was no nation, there was
similarly no need for cities, fortresses and sanctuaries to serve as government agencies.[45]

Evidence from archaeology supports the statement that all the "Levitical"
cities were not instituted at one and the same point in time. All these cities
did not exist in the pre-monarchic time nor in the time of the united Israelite
monarchy. Archaeological remains from the tenth century B.C. have been
found at Beth-Shemesh, Gezer, Gibeon, Ramoth-Gilead (if that is Tell er-
Rumeith), Shechem, and Ta'anak. From the list of Pharaoh Shoshenq concerning his campaign in Palestine we know of the existence of Beth-Horon

---

[43] "The Land Promise is used for etiological purposes to legitimize the possession
of the land." W.M. Clark, *The Origin and Development of the Land Promise Theme in
the Old Testament* (Unpubl. Ph.D. diss., Yale University), New Haven 1964, p. 98. The
Land Promise Theme is not originally a part of the patriarchal tradition, according to
Clark, pp. 55ff. For a discussion about Gen. 15 and 17, see also J. van Seters, *Abraham
in History and Tradition*, New Haven and London 1975, pp. 279ff.

[44] It should be noted that A.G. Auld considers the list of Josh. 21 to be younger
than that of 1 Chr. 6, "The 'Levitical Cities': Text and History," *ZAW* 91/79, pp. 199ff.
J. Wellhausen considered the idea of Levitical cities as a "physical impracticability"
and, therefore, as a late phenomenon, *Prolegomena*, pp. 159f.

[45] In theory it may be concluded that if the "Levitical" cities were part of a government system, they could have come into existence as an institution under Saul. Con-
cerning the discussion about the "Levitical" cities, see, for instance, J. Wellhausen,
Prolegomena, pp. 159f., W.F. Albright, "The List of Levitic Cities," *L. Ginsberg
Jubilee Volume*, New York 1945, pp. 49ff., A. Alt, "Festungen und Levitenorte im
Lande Juda," *KS* II, München 1953, pp. 306ff., B. Mazar, "The Cities of the Priests
and Levites," *SVT* 7, 1960, pp. 195ff., Y. Aharoni, *The Land of the Bible*, pp. 269ff.,
J.L. Peterson, *A Topographical Survey of the Levitical "Cities" of Joshua 21 and
1 Chronicles 6: Studies on the Levites in Israelite Life and Religion* (Unpubl. Th.D.
diss., Seabury Western Theol. Seminary), Evanston, Ill., 1979, J.R. Spencer, *The
Levitical Cities*, 1980.

and Mahanaim.[46] Regarding Heshbon in Transjordan the archaeological picture is still unclear. Because only a few pottery sherds have been found it appears that no major settlement existed there between ca. 1050–900 B.C. The fact that more pottery has been found from the ninth century B.C. may indicate a settlement.[47]

If Ramoth-Gilead is identified with Tell er-Rumeith it came into existence during the tenth century B.C. As mentioned above, no remains dated to the time before the tenth century have been uncovered there.[48]

Another "Levitical" city in Transjordan that should be mentioned is Jahaṣ. It has tentatively been identified with Khirbet el-Medeiyineh[49] or Khirbet Zibb.[50] A recent survey showed that there was no pottery from the eleventh or tenth centuries at these places. Even though a survey cannot give a complete picture of a site's history, it does give an indication of what is probable. The results of the survey of the "Levitical Cities" should be combined with what we know from the Mesha inscription, mid-ninth century B.C. Lines 18f. mention that the Israelite king (probably Omri) built (בנה) Jahaṣ. Because the verb בנה, "to build", is used,[51] it may mean that this was a new city constructed by the Israelites.[52] Therefore, it can be concluded that Jahaṣ did not exist during the period of the Judges and the united monarchy. The building of the city of Jahaṣ can, thus, be seen as an example of urbanization as a political tool.

Other cities labelled "Levitical" include Jutta, Eshtemoa, and Jattir. These three cities were located south of Hebron and may have been part of a defense line. The above mentioned survey of "Levitical Cities" turned up no tenth century pottery there. The earliest settlement at Jattir (probably

---

[46] See W. Helck, *Die Beziehungen Ägyptens*, p. 239, M. Noth, "Die Wege der Pharaonenheere in Palästina und Syrien," *ZDPV* 61/38, pp. 277ff., K.A. Kitchen, *The Third Intermediate Period*, pp. 432ff.

[47] See R.S. Boraas and L.T. Geraty, "Heshbon 1974," *Andrews University Seminary Studies* 14/76, pp. 7f., and J.A. Sauer, *id.*, p. 60, cf. also Geraty, "The 1974 Season of Excavations at Tell Ḥesbân," *Annual of the Department of Antiquities* (Jordan) 20/75, p. 51.

[48] Cf. above, chapter III.

[49] Y. Aharoni, *The Land of the Bible*, pp. 187, 308. F.M. Abel identified it with Khirbet Iskander, *Géographie de la Palestine* II, Paris 1938, p. 354.

[50] J.L. Peterson, *A Topographical Survey*. He sees Kh. el-Medeiyineh as an alternative place. – To get a picture of north Transjordanian settlement problems, consult M. Ibrahim–J.A. Sauer––K. Yassine, "The East Jordan Valley Survey, 1975," *BASOR* 222/76, pp. 41-66. According to this survey, most Bronze Age sites show a continuous occupation in Iron I and II periods. However, at "Iron I sites very little, if any, Iron IA pottery was found," and some of the Iron II sites did not yield any pottery from the Iron I period, p. 56.

[51] Cf. *KAI* II, p. 169, 177.

[52] J.C.L. Gibson translates "fortified", *Textbook of Syrian Semitic Inscriptions* I, Oxford 1971, p. 76.

modern 'Attir), for example, seems to be from the late Iron II period; only one sherd from the eighth century B.C. was found. The picture appears to be the same at Jutta and Eshtemoa.[53] Contrary to Aharoni, this indicates that these three cities were not part of Rehoboam's defense line, 2 Chr. 11: 5-12.[54] The text of the Chronicler does not mention them either. If these three cities really were a part of a defense line they may have come into existence during the time of king Jehoshaphat who, according to 2 Chr. 17: 2,12, stationed garrisons in the cities of Judah and strengthened his defenses by building forts and store cities.

It is doubtful whether one can conclude from 2 Chr. 17:2 that Jehoshaphat of Judah divided his kingdom into twelve districts.[55] Simply because he built store cities and fortresses, 2 Chr. 17:12, does not mean that new district divisions were created. However, 2 Chr. 19:4ff. may indicate that the king did reorganize his administration.[56] This text mentions that Jehoshaphat appointed judges in all the fortified cities of Judah (from Beer-Sheba to the hill country of Ephraim)[57] and established what could be called tribunals in Jerusalem. Religious matters, "all matters of Yahweh" (לכל דבר־ יהוה), were under the chief priest, Amariah, and civil matters or "all the king's matters" (לכל דבר־המלך), were under Zebediah, the nāgīd (chief, governor) over the house of Judah, v. 11.[58] It should be noted that verse 11 states that the Levites were officials of these courts. They were the שטרים, the scribes, officers or commissionaires, of the chief priest and of the governor.

That the Chronicler does not mention the "Levitical" cities during the reign of king Jehoshaphat is significant. If the king indeed reorganized his administration and placed Levites under the command of the chief priest of the Jerusalem temple and others under the supervision of the governor, some reference to the Levites of the "Levitical" cities and how they were affected by the new order, would have been expected. On the one hand, it is

[53] At Eshtemoa Z. Yeivin found five jugs with jewellery from the 10th-9th centuries, "Es-Samo'a (As-Samu')," *IEJ* 21/71, pp. 174f.

[54] *The Land of the Bible*, p. 292. Concerning the fortifications built by Rehoboam, consult G. Beyer, "Das Festungssystem Rehabeams," *ZDPV* 54/31, pp. 113-134, cf. Ahlström, "Is Tell ed-Duweir Ancient Lachish?," *PEQ* 112/80, pp. 8f.

[55] Cf. Y. Aharoni, *The Land of the Bible*, p. 297.

[56] Cf. W.F. Albright, "The Judicial Reform of Jehoshaphat," *Alexander Marx Jubilee Volume*, pp. 61ff., W. Rudolph, *Chronikbücher* (HAT 21), Tübingen 1955, pp. 256ff.

[57] The mention of the hill country of Ephraim may refer to cities (among them Ramah and Mizpah) taken by Abiam and Asa, 1 Kings 15:16ff., 2 Chr. 16:1ff., cf. Y. Aharoni, "The Province-List of Judah," *VT* 9/59, pp. 230f. For Josh. 15: 21ff. as a reference to a district division of Judah, see A. Alt, "Judas Gaue unter Josia," *Palästina-jahrbuch* 21/25, pp. 100-116 (= *KS* II, pp. 276-288), and also the summary discussion by Aharoni, *VT* 9/59, pp. 225ff.

[58] Cf. A. Cody, *A History of Old Testament Priesthood*, pp. 121f.

possible that the new organization did not affect the Levites outside Jerusalem. On the other hand, the Chronicler's complete neglect of the "Levitical" cities here may indicate that they did not yet exist as an institution.

This is supported by 2 Chr. 19:7ff. which states that Jehoshaphat sent high officials ("princes") and Levites to all the cities of Judah in order to "teach" the people the law, *tōrāh*, of Yahweh from the lawbook they carried with them. The narrator reported a common phenomenon but gave to it his own interpretation. Just as every government had to spread its officials over the country, so also Jehoshaphat. However, the Chronicler viewed this phenomenon in the light of his own understanding of the facts. By saying that the Levites had a lawbook from which they taught the people the laws of Yahweh, he made them advocates and teachers of his own time's understanding of religion.[59] The *tōrāh* of his time was used as the yardstick by which he judged the religious and political phenomena of pre-exilic time. In other words, the history of the monarchy is presented as if it were part of the post-exilic Jewish community.

From the above discussion it is clear that the lists in Josh. 21 and 1 Chr. 6 do not refer to an institution of so-called "Levitical" cities that arose during the monarchic period or before.[60] The post-exilic historiographer[61] derived his concept of "Levitical" cities from the old administrative system of appointing, among others, priestly and civil personnel to serve in certain cities. This was especially important in strategical places and newly incorporated areas. In other words, in the historical reconstruction one way of making the different Canaanite areas "Israelite" was to place Levites in them. This was initiated at the beginning of the "settlement" in the country. Therefore, the logical thing to do was to anchor this phenomenon in a decree given by Moses, Nu. 35:1ff.

The list of "Levitical" cities may be seen as a part of the literary activity of the post-exilic time whose aim was to justify the claim on the country. In the historical reconstruction, the fact that Canaan was once under Israelite-

---

[59] G.E. Wright argued that the Levites were sent out as teachers of the *tōrāh*, the law, "The Levites in Deuteronomy," *VT* 4/54, p.329. He is followed by J.L. Peterson, who views the Levites as religious teachers of the Mosaic law. The "Levitical" cities should have become "Yahweh teaching centers," *A Topographical Survey*. The national cult as the main artery of the nation's life is ignored by Wright and Peterson, who make the Levites look like modern teachers of theology and ethics. It should be added that Peterson sees the "Levitical" cities as a north-Israelite phenomenon which came into existence during the time of Jeroboam II, pp. 268f. This does not, however, solve the problem of the "Levitical" cities of Judah.

[60] The so-called Levitical Cities Survey determined that only twenty out of over seventy places surveyed showed any pottery from before the 9th-8th centuries B.C. It should also be mentioned that the majority of them were probably unwalled settlements, see further Peterson, *op. cit.*

[61] Cf. J. Wellhausen, *Prolegomena*, pp. 160f., A.G. Auld, *ZAW* 91/79, pp. 200ff.

Davidic rule played an important role; it was according to the will of Yahweh. The "Levitical" cities phenomenon is to be seen as one expression of this ideology.

Turning to the reign of Jeroboam I it should be noted that his first choice as capital was the ancient city of Shechem, 1 Kings 12:25.[62] It appears that he began to rebuild and fortified it immediately (here the verb בנה is used). It may be assumed that the choice of Shechem was made because it was known as having been an old royal city, and because it had once been a center for the běnē yiśrā'ēl. However, Jeroboam's intention to make Shechem the capital of Israel never materialized. The excavations at Tell Balaṭa (ancient Shechem) show that the place was an insignificant village before Jeroboam's time. There are no remains of a fortified town from the tenth century B.C.[63] Thus, when 1 Kings 12:25 continues by saying that Jeroboam marched from (יצא) Shechem to Penuel in Transjordan and built it (rebuilt?), it may mean that there was no time to build up and fortify Shechem. Because of the political situation Penuel may have been a temporary place of refuge for the new government. According to 1 Kings 15:6, there was an almost permanent state of warfare between Judah and Israel as long as Rehoboam of Judah lived. At a more secure and distant place from the battles with Judah, Jeroboam could better organize his army and government apparatus.[64] Moreover, Penuel was not too far from the Transjordanian sites of iron ore.[65]

A second and perhaps more decisive reason behind the move to Penuel[66] was Pharaoh Shoshenq's campaign in Palestine. This may have posed a threat to all Palestinian states and their independence. It is most probable that Jeroboam did not have time to make Shechem a real stronghold or to build up his war machine because of the advance of the Egyptian army. Thus, in order to avoid a battle with the Egyptians, he left for Penuel and Mahanaim.[67]

---

[62] Here the verb ישב, "to sit, to throne," is used.

[63] G.E. Wright, *Shechem*, pp. 144f., L.E. Toombs, "The Stratigraphy at Tell Balaṭah," *ADAJ* 17/72, pp. 99-110, cf. Toombs, *BASOR* 223/76, pp. 58f., and "Shechem: Problems of the Early Israelite Era," *Symposia*, ed. by F.M. Cross, Cambridge, Mass., 1979, pp. 69ff.

[64] Thus B. Otzen, *Israeliterne i Palaestina*, Copenhagen 1977, p. 212. Cf. the parallel with Eshbaal, Saul's son, making Mahanaim in Transjordan his capital, 2 Sam. 2:8.

[65] Penuel "was the only mining town" within Jeroboam's kingdom, M. Har-el, "The Valley of the Craftsmen (ge' haharašim)," *PEQ* 109/77, p. 85, n. 63.

[66] M. Noth, "Die Schoschenkliste," *ZDPV* 61/38, pp. 277ff., B. Mazar, "The Campaign of Pharaoh Shishak to Palestine," *SVT* 4/57, pp. 57ff., K.A. Kitchen, *The Third Intermediate Period*, pp. 293ff.

[67] Kitchen, *op. cit.*, p. 298, cf. W. Helck, *Die Beziehungen*, p. 239. It has been suggested that the name -rḏ' (or -ru-ṣe') in the Shoshenq list (no.59) be identified with Tirzah. Thus, this city was taken before Jeroboam moved there, so, for instance,

As far as we know, the Egyptian campaign did not result in any lasting land possessions. No texts tell us whether the Palestinian states were reduced or became vassal states. It is possible, though, that the territory of Judah was diminished. That Rehoboam did not rebuild Arad may indicate that it was no longer within the borders of Judah.[68] Whether the Pharaoh wished only to "show the flag" and reclaim respect for Egyptian power[69] or whether he dominated parts of Palestine for a short time is not known. What is clear is that as a result of Solomon's death and Shoshenq's invasion, the Palestinian states were again reduced to nations of little importance. Consequently, Jeroboam moved his residence to Tirzah, 1 Kings 14:7, a city more easily defensible than Shechem because of its geographical location.

According to the Chronicler, when Israel declared its independence, priests and Levites left Israel for Judah and allied themselves with Rehoboam (2 Chr. 11:13f.) because Jeroboam chose others to be priests in the new kingdom.[70] From a political and administrative point of view this is quite natural. Jeroboam could not trust the officials of the old government. Indeed, it is probable that most of them were faithful to Rehoboam. Dissolving the union and making Israel an independent nation, Jeroboam appointed, of course, officials, including priests, who swore allegiance to him alone. Priests and others who were appointed by Solomon's government and who opposed Jeroboam may not have left the new nation of their own free will; it is probable that the new king dismissed them. Because the late historiographer viewed the break between Israel and Judah as a "sin", Jeroboam's act of appointing his own priests was characterized as illegitimate. Naturally, the Chronicler ignored the royal prerogative of appointing priests since it did not suit his theological reconstruction of the history.[71]

It must now be asked why Jeroboam chose Bethel as a royal sanctuary place but did not make it the capital of Israel. Although the biblical text is not informative, it may be assumed that when Shechem was abandoned as

---

B. Mazar, *op. cit.,* p. 60. This identification is, according to Helck, "aus der Luft gegriffen," *op. cit.,* p. 242.

[68] G.W. Ahlström, *PEQ* 112/80, p. 8.

[69] S. Herrmann, *A History of Israel,* p. 197.

[70] N. Allan believes that Jeroboam left Shechem because he came into conflict with the Levites of the city, "Jeroboam and Shechem," *VT* 24/74, pp. 353ff.

[71] For the theological historiography of the Chronicler, see P.R. Ackroyd, "History and Theology in the Writings of the Chronicler," *Concordia Theological Monthly* 38/ 67, pp. 501-515, and "The Age of the Chronicler," (The Selwyn Lectures for 1970 delivered at the College of Saint John the Evangelist, Auckland, New Zealand), *Colloquium* 1970, pp. 43ff. For the evaluation of Jeroboam in 1 Kings 12, see, for instance, H. Donner, who says that "Jeroboam could not have known anything about this Deuteronomic law of centralization... since it came into being only centuries later." "The Separate States of Israel and Judah," in *Israelite and Judean History,* ed. by J.H. Hayes and J.M. Miller, 1977, p. 388.

the capital, Bethel, a prestigiuos cult place in the hill country,[72] was a natural choice for Jeroboam.[73] Because it had been an Israelite cult place long before Jerusalem came into the picture (cf. Gen. 28:10ff.) Jeroboam could advocate that it was closer to the mainstream of Israelite religion than was Jerusalem with its new temple and Zadoqite, non-Israelite priesthood.[74] Therefore, Bethel did not become a national sanctuary because it was close to the border, as has been maintained.[75] Of the three old sanctuaries to which Samuel went once a year, Bethel was the most northern. Of the other two, Mispah was too close to the border with Judah and Gilgal was located too far to the east of the classical Israelite territory.[76] However, also Bethel was located in the southern region of the new kingdom and, thus, dangerously close to Judah.[77]

The textual material is of no help in trying to assess the importance of the city of Bethel under David and Solomon. Unfortunately, there are no references to the city during the time of the united monarchy. However, from archaeology the conclusion may be drawn that Bethel (if it is identified with modern Beitin)[78] was a prosperous city in the beginning of the Iron II period.[79] This may have further induced Jeroboam to make the city a national religious center.

To determine the religious position of Bethel in the new kingdom, one could ask whether it was *the* official cult place of the national religion and its administration. In other words, should Bethel's cult place be compared with Jerusalem's temple? Again the historical texts do not give us an exact answer. However, it is clear that Bethel's sanctuary never became a king's palace sanctuary. Here one should remember that Jeroboam's first task was to make the new nation a viable one, and for that purpose he required an

---

[72] Cf. F.F. Hvidberg, *Weeping and Laughter in the Old Testament,* Leiden and Copenhagen 1962, pp. 85ff., E. Nielsen, *Shechem,* p. 307, F.M. Cross, *Canaanite Myth and Hebrew Epic,* pp. 199, 279.

[73] If the Danite priesthood at the time of Jeroboam long claimed descendance from an ancestoral hero, Moses (Judg. 17-18), it is understandable why Jeroboam elevated Dan's temple to the status of a royal sanctuary.

[74] Cf. Ahlström, "Der Prophet Nathan und der Tempelbau," *VT* 11/61, pp. 113ff., and "Was David a Jebusite Subject?," *ZAW* 92/80, pp. 286f.

[75] Y. Aharoni, *BA* 31/68, p. 28.

[76] Cf. H. Motzki, "Ein Beitrag zum Problem des Stierkultes in der Religionsgeschichte Israel," *VT* 25/75, p. 474.

[77] King Abijam of Judah incorporated Bethel with his kingdom, according to 2 Chr. 13:19. It is not known under which Israelite king Bethel was retaken (Baasha?).

[78] D. Livingstone identifies the modern Birah with ancient Bethel, "Location of Biblical Bethel and Ai Reconsidered," *The Westminster Theological Journal* 33/70, pp. 20ff. For a critique of Livingstone's theory, see A.F. Rainey, "Bethel is still Beitin," *The Westminster Theological Journal* 33/60, pp. 175ff.

[79] W.F. Albright and J.L. Kelso, *The Excavation of Bethel (1934–1960)* (AASOR 39), 1968, pp. 36f., and 50.

efficient administration. From 1 Kings 11:28 we learn that Jeroboam had been one of Solomon's chief administrators. As such, he was in charge of the levy of the "house of Joseph," and occupied one of the most prominent positions in the northern part of the nation, i.e. the part which later became his kingdom. Consequently, he was well acquainted with the districts, their functions and the religious duties of their officials. It should not be assumed that the district organization ceased to function when Solomon died and the united monarchy was split. Thus, Jeroboam had an organization to fall back on. This does not mean that the forced labor system continued exactly as before. The new king must certainly have made some changes in this respect.[80] Indeed, not to have done so would have meant running the risk of a revolution. One thing that Jeroboam had to decide quickly was where to locate an official center for the new nation's official religion and cult administration – a place where the king himself could fullfil his religious duties. Although he chose Bethel, whether or not the choice was meant to be temporary is unknown. In his reorganization of the new nation's cultic calendar the king had to institute a royal festival at Bethel in which he himself was to officiate. This festival was naturally patterned after the royal festival of Jerusalem, 1 Kings 12:32.[81] It is, thus, a possibility that Jeroboam intended to make Bethel his capital but soon found it strategically unsuitable.

Bethel, however, kept its status as a royal temple place. This is clear from Amos 7:13 where the (chief) priest, Amaziah, tells the Judean prophet Amos that he is forbidden to deliver his "dangerous" oracles at Bethel because it is a king's sanctuary, מקדש מלך, and a temple of the kingdom, בית ממלכה. Amos, who was not an Israelite citizen, threatened the life of the king and his dynasty, 7:7-9. To do so on royal property was understood as instigating a revolt, 7:10f. As a citizen of another nation it was natural to expel him and order him back to his own country, Judah.

The two above mentioned phrases may not be exact synonyms. מקדש מלך designates both royal property and a temple where the king himself could officiate, as did Jeroboam, 1 Kings 12:32f. The other phrase, בית ממלכה, may refer to any other sanctuary that belonged to the nation's official religion and was, as such, part of the royal administrative system.[82] The sanc-

---

[80] Some district governors were probably replaced, as those who were Solomon's sons-in-law.

[81] Cf. E. Nielsen, *Shechem*, p. 277, Ahlström, *Psalm 89*, pp. 93f.

[82] If בית ממלכה was the common term for a state temple it may be asked why its use is not more frequent in the Old Testament. The reason may be that in a later time the term *bāmāh* became the technical and derogatory term for the sanctuaries outside Jerusalem. Because the biblical narrators were in favor of the Jerusalem temple cult and considered it the only Yahweh temple where the nation's god could be worshipped with sacrifices, these other cult places could not be mentioned as official sanctuaries. Thus, the word *bāmāh* seems to have served their polemical purpose. For the *bāmāh* problem, see W. Boyd Barrick, *The Word BMH in the Old Testament* (Unpubl. Ph.D.

tuaries mentioned in 1 Kings 12:31 and 2 Kings 23:19 may be examples of the second category (they are called *bāmôt* by the later historiographer). It should be noted that the latter passage mentions that the kings of Israel built בתי הבמות in their kingdom.[83] These, then, were sanctuaries of the kingdom, ממלכה .

The characterization given to Bethel in Am. 7:13 shows that it still was a temple of higher rank than an ordinary בית ממלכה . How its status compared with the sanctuary of the royal establishment in Samaria is unknown. As usual the narrators do not tell us the whole story. Their interest in Israel is doctrinal throughout, not historical.[84] Thus, neither Tirzah nor Samaria are pictured as religious centers. However, because every capital was the center for the government's religious affairs, the narrators did not need to emphasize this phenomenon. It was natural to expect a temple or a royal chapel within the palace complexes of these two cities. Even if the leadership of the national religion was centered in the capitals, Bethel's importance as a national cult place was very strong and continued to be so even after the collapse of the kingdom of Israel. This is shown by the fact that the Assyrian king (which one is not said) sent one of the exiled priests back to Bethel and not to Samaria to ensure that the religion of the country was carried out efficiently, according to its norms, *mišpāṭ*, 2 Kings 17:26ff.

It should be noted that Bethel's temple is called a במה in 2 Kings 23:15.[85] This text states that king Josiah of Judah broke down the *bāmāh* and burned it together with the Asherah. The RSV translation of this verse is noteworthy; the "altars with the high place he pulled down and he broke in pieces its stones, crushing them to dust; also he burned the Asherah." The Hebrew text, however, says something else. It has וישרף את־הבמה which can only be translated "he burned the *bāmāh*." Thus, *bāmāh* cannot possibly mean the altar, as proposed by P.H. Vaughan,[86] but must be understood as something made of wood or partly of wood, probably a building. The reason why the word *bāmāh* is used for the temple of Bethel is that the writer, who favored Josiah's religious and political activities, regarded only

---

diss., University of Chicago), Chicago 1977. P.H. Vaughan, *The Meaning of 'bāmâ' in the Old Testament*, Cambridge 1972, is not fully convincing.

[83] Cf. Barrick, *op. cit.*, pp. 326f. H. Torzyner (Tur-Sinai) says that he "tried to show that 'bamot' are not 'high places', but sacred buildings on both high as in low places," *Lachish I: The Lachish Letters*, Oxford 1938, p. 30, n. 3.

[84] H. Tadmor prefers to see Samaria as a secular city and not as a center for the nation's religion. "On the History of Samaria in the Biblical Period," *Eretz Shomron*, Jerusalem 1972, pp. 67ff. (Hebrew). However, the narrators have played down the role of Samaria as an official Yahweh cult place because of their principal opposition to the existence of Israel as a nation. Because the archaeological material thus far available is incomplete, a true picture of the city's religious establishment cannot be drawn.

[85] Cf. E. Nielsen, *Shechem*, p. 197.

[86] *The Meaning of 'bāmâ' in the Old Testament*, p. 32f.

one Yahweh temple as legitimate, Jerusalem's. Thus, he used his own devaluating term for Bethel's temple. No longer a royal cult place, Bethel was nothing more than one among many cult places in the (now crumbling) Assyrian empire. However, as an important Yahwistic holy place in the province of Samerina, it was still an important competitor to the Solomonic temple for the zealous Jerusalemite writer.[87]

From what has been said above, it is probable that both Tirzah and Samaria had a sanctuary or a chapel in the royal quarter or in the palace itself.[88] Indeed, at some point, Samaria may have rivalled Bethel as a cult

---

[87] It is possible that the utterances in Am. 9:1 and 1 Kings 13:2 are prophecies *ex eventu* which must be understood in the light of 2 Kings 23:15. If Am. 9:1 is a prophecy *ex eventu* it may be concluded that the book of Amos was composed in its present form after king Josiah's destruction of Bethel's temple. Another indication for this is Am. 9:12 which mentions the שארית אדום, "that what is left of Edom." According to the prophecy, the people of Yahweh will take possession of the remnant of Edom. Such an oracle cannot have been pronounced during the mid-eighth century B.C. when Edom was a Judean vassal state, cf. 2 Kings 16:6. Under such a political situation the oracle would have been meaningless for the people of the northern kingdom. Is then Am. 9:11ff. secondary? It depends upon how one looks at the problem of composition. Although it is probable that these words were not spoken by the prophet, the passage may very well be an original part of a literary composition. R.A. Carlson has advocated that Am. 9:7-15 is a compositional counterpart to 1:2–2:16, "Profeten Amos och Davidsriket," *Religion och Bibel* 25/66, pp. 74f. No objections will be raised here. However, this does not necessarily mean that the composition of the book is from the time of the prophet or made by the prophet himself. It may be concluded that the composer, living some hundred years after the prophet, used an Amos-tradition which he reinterpreted in order to speak to the people of his own time (ca 500 B.C.?), a time when Edom was falling apart. This was also the time when the Judahites tried to reorganize themselves. The composer of the book of Amos is advocating the right of the Judahites to the old country. In his propaganda he goes back to the model of the Davidic kingdom, the ideal kingdom which was willed by Yahweh. The harmony that exists between the end of the book of Joel, 4:18ff. (also from ca. 500 B.C., see G.W. Ahlström, *Joel and the Temple Cult of Jerusalem*, Leiden 1971, pp. 120ff.) and the end of Amos, 9:11ff. should be noted. Both mention Edom in a hostile manner (cf. Obadiah, and Ezek. 25:12ff., 35:1ff.) and both mention the ideal time to come for the people of Yahweh, cf. H.W. Wolff, *Amos* (BK XIV), p. 406.

[88] E.L. Sukenik found the remains of what he called an "Israelite shrine" outside the city of Samaria, see J.W. Crowfoot, K.M. Kenyon, E.L. Sukenik, *Samaria-Sebaste I. The Buildings of Samaria*, London 1942, pp. 23f. and fig. 11. However, nothing indicates that this structure was a sanctuary. Sukenik's conclusion is based on the "immense quantity of pottery... coupled with the extraordinary lay-out of the whole structure," p. 24. The quantity of pottery is, however, no decisive factor for determining a place as being a shrine. The structure, which is a trench, seems to be uncompleted. Because some cuttings in it have the form of, for instance, a dromos, a cave, or a tumulus, one may suspect that the purpose of cutting the trench was to make a burial place, which was never finished. It is namely possible that this "structure is post-Israelite. Some of the figurines found in it have been dated to ca. 725–700 B.C., cf. T.A. Holland, "A Study of Palestinian Iron Age Baked Clay Figurines, with special Relevance to Jerusalem: Cave I," *Levant* 9/77, p. 148.

center. That a sanctuary existed there is indicated by Hosea's above mentioned reference to the "calf" of Samaria, 8:5f. which may be the prophet's tendentious term for the cultic establishment of the capital.[89] Therefore, this holy place cannot be identified with the temple king Ahab built for his Tyrian queen, Jezebel, and her entourage. Dedicated to the Tyrian Baal, 1 Kings 16:32, a god not to be identified with the indigenous Baal of the territory of Israel, the temple was constructed because the queen had to worship her own god in the new and strange country to which she had come. Thus, her temple was not a "Reichstempel" but should, phenomenologically, be viewed as a parallel to the sanctuaries Solomon built for his foreign wifes.[90] As it turned out, Jezebel's Baal temple competed for a time with the official cultic establishment of Samaria. This means that there must have been an official Yahweh sanctuary in the city.[91] Indeed, it would have been an exception to the rule in the ancient Near East to have a capital without a sanctuary as the center of the royal administration's religious affairs.[92]

We learn very little about the royal administration in the northern kingdom, Israel, and its supervision of the cult. Because of their ideological orientation, the narrators had no cause to detail such matters. As a break

---

[89] Contra H.W. Wolff, *Hosea* (BK XIV:1), pp. 179f. (Engl. ed. p. 140). Wolff maintains that Jezebel's Baal temple did not exist at the time of the prophet Hosea. However, he views Hosea's reference to the calf of Samaria as a reference to the bull at Bethel. But, as Wolff himself states, the prophet talks to the inhabitants of Samaria, a term that comprised an area no greater than the city of Samaria. It is thus the idol of the capital of Israel about which Hosea speaks.

[90] Cf. G.W. Ahlström, "King Jehu – A Prophet's Mistake," *Scripture in History and Theology,* Essays in Honor of J.C. Rylaarsdam, Pittsburg, 1977, p. 52.

[91] N. Noth postulated that Samaria had its own royal sanctuary in which "probably a 'golden calf' was erected," *The History of Israel,* p. 232 (German 3rd ed., p. 212). Whether or not the calf was a symbol of the Canaanite-Israelite Baal or Yahweh, is never stated in the texts. The latter would, however, be the most probable in view of 1 Kings 12 (cf. Ex. 32), see also the personal name עגליו on an ostracon from Samaria (no. 41), D. Diringer, *Le iscrizioni antico-ebraiche palestinesi,* Firenze 1934, pp. 32, 39f. Concerning 1 Kings 12:26ff. one must admit that it would have been impossible for Jeroboam I to present Yahweh to the people in the form of a bull image if he never had been worshipped in that form before, cf. E. Nielsen, *Shechem,* p. 277, G.W. Ahlström, *Psalm 89,* pp. 93f. For a discussion of the fact that Yahweh was long identified with bull – El of Canaan, cf. J.P. Brown, "The Sacrificial Cult and its Critique in Greek and Hebrew (I)," *JSS* 24/79, pp. 167ff. This is what Hosea opposes in his criticism of the cults of Bethel and Samaria. He calls the god Baal instead of Yahweh, thus twisting the fact. One should also note that Elijah, for instance, opposed neither bull worship nor the existence of such cult paraphernalia as *maṣṣēbôt* and *'ăšērîm,* I. Engnell, *A Rigid Scrutiny,* ed. by J.T. Willis, Nashville 1969, p. 132. For the cult of the 'calf' as an old Israelite cultform, see also S. Talmon, "Divergences in Calendar Reckoning in Ephraim and Judah," *VT* 8/58, p. 50.

[92] L.R. Fisher assumes that there was "more than one temple quarter in Samaria," "The Temple Quarter," *JSS* 8/63, p. 38, n. 1.

away from Yahweh of Jerusalem and the Davidic dynasty, the northern kingdom should not have existed. Indeed, from the narrator's vantage point, a northern kingdom could do only what "was evil in the eyes of Yahweh." One may assume, however, that the district organization Jeroboam I inherited[93] and the administrative apparatus he must have instituted continued with perhaps some necessary adjustments. In connection with Ahab, for example, we learn about the governors of the districts, 1 Kings 20:14f. That the kings were the masters of the nation's cultic affairs is evident from the reigns of, among others, Ahab and Joram.[94] Not only did Ahab have the above mentioned temple built for his queen, but he also erected a stele to Baal in Samaria, 2 Kings 3:2. That his son Joram ejected it may be seen as a reaction against a god who was not originally part of the national religion of the country. If so, this Baal stele was probably a symbol for the Tyrian Baal.[95] Joram's removal of this stele may indicate that he was more of a traditionalist and, thus, did not strongly support the queen mother's activities in religious matters.

Jehu's slaughter of Yahweh priests and the priests of the Tyrian Baal cult, 2 Kings 10:11, reveals that his revolt was basically political and did not reflect any religious disaffection. To firmly establish his position he killed not only the whole house of the Omrides but all who were politically allied with it as well. In this way the anti-Assyrian politics of Israel were terminated. The pro-Egyptian party was put out of function.[96] Jehu's revolt suited the narrator of 2 Kings who gave to it a specific religious color, as if it were in harmony with his time's concept of Yahwism. Nevertheless, he complains about Jehu, 2 Kings 10:29ff., as he does about all the kings of Israel. They followed in the footsteps of Jeroboam I. How Jehu's administration dealt with religious matters is not really known. It may be concluded, however, that the official religion of Israel continued in its traditional forms now freed from Tyrian competition.

Concerning Judah, the biblical writers considered the cultic reforms of the Judahite kings Asa and his son Jehoshaphat, to be in harmony with their

---

[93] Cf. J. Bright, *A History of Israel*, p. 233. The Samaria ostraca from the eighth century B.C. have also been seen as an indication for the existence of a district organization of the northern kingdom, see among others, Y. Aharoni, *The Land of the Bible*, pp. 315-327, W.H. Shea, "The Date and Significance of the Samaria Ostraca," *IEJ* 27/77, pp. 16-77 (with lit.). Concerning the importance of the ostraca also for Hebrew grammar, see A.F. Rainey, "The Samaria Ostraca in the Light of Fresh Evidence," *PEQ* 99/67, pp. 32-41.

[94] For the religious situation under the Omrides, see my article, "King Jehu – A Prophet's Mistake," pp. 47-69.

[95] Ahlström, *op. cit.*, p. 53.

[96] *Id.* pp. 47ff.

ideals, 1 Kings 15, 22:41, 2 Chr. 14-17.[97] Both kings attempted to put an
end to cultic prostitution in the country and in Jerusalem.[98] However, because they are blamed for not having stopped the cult of the *bāmôt*, their
"reforms" cannot be seen as part of a contemporary movement desirous of
reforming the national cult of Judah. No thought had yet been given to the
idea of cult centralization in Jerusalem. The conclusion one can draw from
the biblical texts is that both kings certainly made changes in cultic affairs,
and because the later writers appreciated these actions they were seen as
examples of "righteous" rulers.

According to 2 Kings 12:5-17 ‖ 2 Chr. 24:4-11, king Joash of Judah,
who ascended the throne after the coup against queen Athaliah, tried to collect money in order to restore the temple of Solomon. Although he ordered
the first priest, Jehoiadah, to send priests and Levites to the cities of the
nation to collect money for the work, 2 Chr. 24:4ff., the project was
obviously hindered by Jehoiadah for 22 years, 2 Kings 12:6. After a rebuke
by the king, however, he made a chest into which all the money brought to
the temple was deposited, and work began. The reign of queen Athaliah is
viewed as a time of neglect of the Solomonic temple and in some ways it
was. Naturally, she was more interested in her own newly built temple for
the Tyrian Baal. For example, according to 2 Chr. 24:7, the sons of Athaliah
(which may refer to her servants as well) are said to have broken into the
temple of Yahweh and taken vessels from it for use in the new Baal temple.

Two things should be noted here. First, that the chief priest showed such
great reluctance to collect money for the temple indicates that it was not in
a bad state of repair. Second, as long as the priest lived, the king did "what
was right in the eyes of Yahweh." When the priest died, however, Joash is
said to have followed other gods. He is also accused of taking money from
the temple in order to pay tribute to the Arameans. This is given as an
excuse for his murder, 2 Chr. 24:17-25.[99] According to the Chronicler's
theological ideal, the Priest is the one who should lead the king, not vice
versa! Thus, only when Jehoiadah was alive could Joash have done anything
praiseworthy.[100] This is adapted historiography, i.e. information is dis-

---

[97] From the time of king Asa we hear about a levy on the whole population of
Judah, "none was exempt," 1 Kings 15:22. Whether or not this gave Asa the oppor-
tunity to start his religious "reform" is not known, but it should not be considered
impossible.

[98] For Asa demoting Maacha from her official position as kingmother, *gĕbîrāh*,
and destroying the cult symbol she had made for Asherah, see my book, *Aspects of
Syncretism in Israelite Religion*, pp. 57-63.

[99] Cf. 2 Kings 12:17ff. which does not have the information about Jehoiadah's
death.

[100] Cf. R. Mosis, *Untersuchungen zur Theologie des chronistischen Geschichts-
werkes* (Freiburger Theologische Studien 29), Freiburg-Basel-Wien 1973, p. 181.

torted to reflect the writer's preconceived idea of what should have taken place.

The Chronicler's version of the reign of king Uzziah of Judah should be noted. It is the positive aspects of a king's reign that determine how he is evaluated and how the material is arranged.[101] Thus, the Chronicler hails Uzziah as one of the most successful kings of Judah. He was both a warrior and a builder.[102] According to the narrator, however, because he became leprous he must have done something wrong. Therefore, it is said that "his heart grew high to destruction" and that he was false to Yahweh. The only "sin" the narrator can pin on the king is that he burned incense to Yahweh on the altar of incense, 26:16. However, that may be, the Chronicler is writing in a time when there was no king in Judah and when the tensions between kingship and priesthood were a thing of the past. Since the Chronicler, ideologically, is a representative of a desacralized kingship, his report of Uzziah's "sin", i.e. his sacrifice, is but a poor excuse for the king's sickness.[103] Kings were heads of state and, as such, they were leaders of the national religion and they could fulfill some cultic duties (cf. Saul, David, Solomon, Jeroboam, Ahaz). They could also make changes in the cultic festivals and appoint the priests of the national sanctuaries. Uzziah, as the top official of his nation's religion, had the right to sacrifice. In this case, however, he could not do it because he had become leprous; in other words he was cultically unclean.[104]

Administrative and cultic reforms

King Hezekiah is well known for the drastic changes he made in cultic matters.[105] According to 2 Kings 18:4, he "removed" the bāmôt of the kingdom of Judah, broke the maṣṣēbôt, cut the 'ăšērîm, and smashed the bronze serpent, Nehushtan, another divine symbol. In connection with passover-maṣṣôt, he organized a festival of such dimensions that it is said

---

[101] For instance, Rehoboam could not have done anything praiseworthy after his first three years as king. It is said that for three years king and people walked "in the way of David and Solomon," 2 Chr. 11:17, P. Welten, *Geschichte und Geschichtsdarstellung in den Chronikbüchern* (WMANT 42), Neukirchen 1973, pp. 42ff.

[102] Uzziah is said to have successfully fought the Philistines and the Arabs; the Ammonites paid him tribute. He should also have built cities on conquered Philistine territory, 2 Chr. 26:6ff.

[103] Cf. H.H. Rowley, *Worship in Ancient Israel*, Philadelphia 1967, p. 95.

[104] H.W.F. Saggs misunderstood this and maintained that Uzziah attempted "to usurp the prerogatives claimed by the Aaronic Priesthood," *The Encounter with the Divine in Mesopotamia and Israel*, London 1978, p. 163.

[105] For the different opinions about the political circumstances and the reform of Hezekiah, see H.H. Rowley, "Hezekiah's Reform and Rebellion," *BJRL* 44/61-62, pp. 381-431.

that "there had been nothing like this in Jerusalem" since Solomon's time, 2 Chr. 30:26.[106]

The *bāmôt* are the national shrines of the country. Just as king Josiah later "removed", הסיר, the בתי הבמות which were in the province of Samerina and which 2 Kings 23:19 states were built in the cities by the kings of Israel, so too the *bāmôt* "removed" by Hezekiah were state sanctuaries. They should not be placed in the same category as the cult places the people made for themselves under every green tree and in the valleys, cult places the prophets complain about.

What happened to these *bāmôt*, sanctuaries? According to 2 Kings 18:4, the cult paraphernalia called *maṣṣēbôt*, "pillars", and *'ǎšērîm*, i.e. the symbol for the goddess Asherah, were broken (*šbr*), cut down or cut to pieces (*krt*). The *bāmôt*, however, were not destroyed, they were "removed" (*swr* in hiph.), abandoned. It may be that Hezekiah changed the function of these sanctuaries; they ceased to be part of the royal administration and its jurisdiction. In other words, they ceased to exist as national sanctuaries. That Hezekiah did not remove the priests from these cult places may mean that they had to rely on other means to earn their living. Even if the sanctuaries were cut off from being part of the royal administration they were probably not destroyed;[107] the text of 2 Kings 18:4 does not say anything to that effect. In 2 Kings 21:3 it is, however, said that Manasseh (re)built (וַיִּבֶן) the *bāmôt* that his father had given up (אבד in pi., a term which does not always mean "destroy"). The use of the verb *bnh* in this connection may refer either to Manasseh having rebuilt the sanctuaries or to the narrator's interpretation of the event. He may have seen the reinstitution of the Judahite cult not only as a reconsecration but also as referring to building activities. Thus, when 2 Chr. 33:17 mentions that during the time of Manasseh the people again sacrificed at the *bāmôt* it means that the official Yahweh cult of Judah was once again administered all over the nation.[108]

What led Hezekiah to undertake his reorganization is not known, but political and economic reasons may have played some role in his decision.[109] It could perhaps be seen as part of his fortification program and part of his foreign policy reversal.[110] With the support of Egypt, he worked for an alliance against the Assyrians. In centralizing everything to the capital, cf.

---

[106] One may conclude that the passover had not been an important festival during the monarchic time.

[107] The Chronicler has here used the verb *ntṣ*, "pull down, break down," which is in harmony with his conceptions and interpretation of history.

[108] See below, Chapter V.

[109] For cult reorganizations in connection with royal building activities, see P. Welten, *Geschichte und Geschichtsdarstellung in den Chronikbüchern*, pp. 180ff.

[110] Cf. M. Weinfeld, "Cult Centralization in Israel in the Light of a Neo-Babylonian Analogy," *JNES* 23/64, pp. 202ff.

2 Chr. 31:10ff., he got all the taxes sent directly to Jerusalem. From there he distributed the goods to the priests and the Levites of the cities of Judah, 2 Chr. 31:14ff. One should, thus, not underestimate the role economy played in Hezekiah's reform program. In order to efficiently stop the cult at the national sanctuaries and their economic importance the king had to erradicate their divine symbols, the maṣṣēbôt and the 'ăšērim. In this way he made it impossible to carry out further rituals as well as collecting tithes at these places.[111]

From a religio-political point of view several of Hezekiah's contemporaries could maintain that the termination of the official cult at the bāmôt was a disastrous move[112] since it decreased the power of the god of the nation, Yahweh, and thus the power of the nation itself. According to Semitic thinking, the king's action undermined his own position. This should be kept in mind when dealing with the reign of king Manasseh who reversed his father's policies.[113] This interpretation is supported by the information given in 2 Kings 18:22 and Isa. 36:7. Here, in a speech directed to the people of Jerusalem[114] (most of them were undoubtedly soldiers), the Assyrian official, rabšāqēh, mentions that Hezekiah's abandonment of the bāmôt and altars of Yahweh had a negative effect. It became dangerous to rely upon Yahweh since his power had been frightfully diminished.[115] As we know, Hezekiah's policies also led the country to the brink of disaster. Most of the territory of Judah was given over to the Philistines by Senna-

---

[111] The phrase עבודת בית האלהים, "The work of the house of God," which occurs in the short evaluation statement about Hezekiah, 2 Chr. 31:21, may refer to the cult of the temple, the liturgy. It is found in parallelism with תורה and מצוה, law and commandments. Concerning the reasons for the so called reform the Oriental Institute Prism Col. III: 38f. mention that lúurbi and lúdamquti were brought into Jerusalem by Hezekiah. The damqūti refers to soldiers and urbi may thus also refer to people used as irregular soldiers, see the discussion by I. Eph'al, "'Arabs' in Babylonia in the eight century B.C.," JAOS 94/74, p. 110. One may ask whether the urbi were ordinary men who were "drafted" in order to strenghthen the defense of Jerusalem. This could have meant that all activities outside the capital almost came to a halt including cultic activities. If so, the biblical narrator may have used and developed this in this report of the "reform," thus giving a tendentious picture of it.

[112] For a possible prophetic opposition to Hezekiah's reform, cf. Weinfeld, op. cit., pp. 208ff.

[113] See further below, Chapter V.

[114] H. Wildberger maintains that the tradition in 2 Kings 18 is taken over by the writer of Isa. 36-39 who revised it, "Die Rede des Rabsake vor Jerusalem," ThZ 35/79, pp. 35-47.

[115] It may be maintained that the rabšāqēh speech is a literary propaganda product, as is the Cyrus cylinder's reference to Nabunaid's transfer of Babylonian gods to Babylon shortly before Cyrus took the city. Still, there may be a kernel of truth in both stories, cf. the discussion by M. Weinfeld, JNES 23/64, pp. 202ff. For an Assyrian parallel to the rabšāqēh's negotiations with the people of a besieged city, see H.W.F. Saggs, "The Nimrud Letters, 1952 – Part I," Iraq 17/55, pp. 23ff.

cherib. Only Jerusalem was left (perhaps also the Judean desert) for Hezekiah to rule.[116] In reality the kingdom of Judah had been reduced to a city state.

The fact that the *rabšāqēh* spoke Hebrew may indicate that he was an Israelite by birth.[117] The aim of his words was to encourage criticism and opposition to Hezekiah's actions. Indeed, to a great many people Hezekiah's actions against their cult places may have been impossible to comprehend. From the *rabšāqēh*'s speech it is evident that the *bāmôt* and altars idled by the reform were seen as legitimate Yahweh cult places.[118] Further, they were not identical phenomena. Opposition to these arose at a later time and came from a group that had accepted and also propagated the idea of only one Yahweh cult place.

The reforms of Hezekiah seem to have been repeated by king Josiah. Both did something to the *bāmôt*, both destroyed *maṣṣēbôt* and *'ăšērîm*, and both inaugurated a new festival in the spring. Josiah is said to have made a passover, the likes of which had not been celebrated since the days of the Judges. It was held for the first time in the king's 18th year, 2 Kings 23:22.[119] Because the narratives in 2 Kings 18 and 23 are similar, it is difficult to establish what exactly happened.

One difference should, however, be pointed out immediately. Josiah is not said to have "removed" the *bāmôt* of Judah. He is said to have "defiled" (ויטמא) the *bāmôt* of the cities, 23:9, because incense was burned there to Baal and the constellations, i.e. the heavenly host.[120] Moreover, he deposed those priests who fulfilled this function, namely the כמרים.[121] Thus, a certain class of priests was dismissed.[122] 2 Kings 23:9 reveals that other priests were not completely put out of business. This verse states that the *bāmôt*-priests could not go up "to the altar of Yahweh in Jerusalem unless they had eaten unleavened bread among their breathren." The phrase כי אם־אכלו gives the condition[123] under which they were permitted to officiate at the

---

[116] See Chapter V.

[117] H. Tadmor sees him as an exiled Israelite who made a career in the Assyrian army, as did many other men of subjugated peoples (in a lecture at the University of Chicago, June 1977).

[118] Cf. M. Weinfeld, *op. cit.*, p. 202, W.B. Barrick, *The Word BMH in the Old Testament*, p. 325.

[119] Either this means that the festival was a new one, or that the old spring festival was "revised." It could also mean that the narrator considered the Josian festival to be in harmony with his own time's passover.

[120] One wonders how this affected the concept of Yahweh as Zebaoth, "Yahweh of Hosts."

[121] This word does not mean "idolatrous" priests, as the Engl. translation renders it. The stem *kmr* means "to be hot, to burn." These priests are said to have been appointed by the kings of Judah, 2 Kings 23:5. Their cultic duties were thus part of the official Judahite religion until the time of Josiah.

[122] See W.B. Barrick, *The Word BMH*, pp. 332f.

[123] C. Brockelmann, *Hebräische Syntax*, Neukirchen 1956, §168, pp. 159f., Bar-

altar of the temple of Jerusalem. From this W.B. Barrick concluded that the *bāmôt*-priests were put "under the control of the Temple priesthood" at Jerusalem.[124]

By changing the status of the national cult places, the *bāmôt*, by dismissing priests, and by subjecting the rest of the priesthood to more direct Jerusalemite temple control[125] the supervision of cultic affairs was tightened. If this story is accurate, the Jerusalemite priesthood gained the upperhand in the struggle between the different priest classes. This may be what started the so called Levitical problem.[126]

Not only did Josiah remove from the Jerusalem temple all the vessels made for Asherah, Baal, and the constellations (the heavenly host), 2 Kings 23:4, but he also removed the horses which the kings of Judah (sic!) had made for the sun, and he burned the chariots of the sun, v.11. Further, he stopped the sacral prostitution at the Solomonic temple, v.7. Here the narrator has provided a clear but short review of the real official religion of the kingdom of Judah. In addition to the three main deities Yahweh Zebaoth, Asherah, and Baal the people has, thus, also worshiped the heavenly bodies. The logic of this is, of course, that there was no monotheism. This is a later speculative idea.[127]

To conclude, as is usually done, that king Manasseh introduced foreign cult phenomena and foreign gods some of which are said to have been eliminated by Josiah, is contrary to textual information. The phrase "the kings of Judah" (who made the horses for the sun) reveals the status of the official and traditional religion of the kingdom. When Yahweh alone remained of the gods after Josiah's purge of the cult the content of the phrase "Yahweh Zebaoth" (Yahweh of Hosts) must have sounded somewhat empty — at least for the time being.[128] If one considers Ezekiel's vision of the twenty-five men worshiping the sun on the inner court of the temple, it appears

---

rick, *op. cit.*, pp. 329f.

[124] *Op. cit.*, pp. 329f.

[125] The details of the government's control of priests and other civil servants escapes us.

[126] Deuteronomy tries to solve this problem. The statutes and directions concerning the Levites are put back in time by assigning them as a part of the Mosaic legislation. In this way the Deuteronomistic legislator got the authority for what he wanted to see as "law." — For the "Law of Deuteronomy" (Chaps. 12–26) as "a unified masterpiece of jurisprudential literature created by a single author, an author who combined ancient civil and cultic regulations with international civil reforms," wisdom, teaching, etc., see the well argumented article by S.A. Kaufman, "The structure of the Deuteronomic Law," *Maarav* 1/79, pp. 105-158 (quote from p. 147). This law code I see as a program for the reconstruction of the post-exilic society.

[127] Because the narrator makes clean sweep and states that everything but Yahweh disappears, it may be suspected that he read more into the reform than actually happened.

[128] A later time gave the phrase a more "angelic" content.

that the worship of the sun was reinstated after Josiah's death, Ezek.
8:16.[129] On the other hand it may be maintained that, even if Josiah re-
jected all the symbols of the sun, the temple rituals may still have included
a *proskynesis* for the sun which the prophet tells us was identified with
Yahweh.[130]

As was mentioned above, Josiah did not destroy the *bāmôt* of Judah nor
did he "remove" (abandon) them from the nation's cultic establishment.
They were perhaps more closely supervised from now on.[131] Certain rituals
were abandoned and the priests performing them, the *kmrm* were dismissed.
There were, however, certain *bāmôt* (here one should perhaps read the
singular *bmh* or *bmt*[132]) which the king did pull down, נתץ. This was the
bmt of the שערים,[133] which was located at "the entrance of the gate of
Joshua, the commander of the city" to the left of the city gate, 2 Kings
23:8. To what city this refers is debated. It has usually been identified as
Jerusalem.[134] However, the sentence ונתץ את במות, "and he pulled down
the *bmt*", may refer to Beer-Sheba.[135] This is supported by 2 Chr. 24:6.
Here Josiah's reform is reported to have included "the cities of Manasseh,
Ephraim, and Simeon, and as far as Naphtali." Beer-Sheba was in the territory of Simeon, the only area of Judah which is mentioned in this passage.
From Am. 5:5 we know that Beer-Sheba was a renowned pilgrimage place
for the people of the northern kingdom, Israel. Connecting this with the
fact that Josiah destroyed the sanctuaries of the former kingdom of Israel
(now the Assyrian province Samerina), it may be concluded that everything
associated with the religious customs of the former northern kingdom was
suspect in the eyes of Josiah and had to be uprooted. The gods of the above
mentioned cult place at Beer-Sheba were not to be associated with Yahweh

---

[129] This is another example of the conservative character of religious life and of
the difficulty of changing rituals and beliefs through a government decree. Ezekiel's
vision cannot be a pure fabrication, since visions are usually built upon some realities.

[130] According to Psalm 84:12 Yahweh is called שמש , "sun." For phenomena of
light and sunshine connected with the character of Yahweh, cf. G.W. Ahlström, *Psalm
89*, pp. 85ff. For Yahweh's horses, see Hab. 3:8.

[131] This may suit the theory of W.E. Claburn who opines that the reform was
mainly a fiscal one, "The Fiscal Basis of Josiah's Reforms," *JBL* 92/73, pp. 11-22.

[132] Cf. W.B. Barrick, *The World BMH*, p. 351.

[133] J. Gray prefers to read *šō'ărîm*, "gatekeepers" which he sees as "guardian
genii" possibly in the form of the Assyrian "bull-colossi," *I & II Kings*, p. 730. For the
reading שעירים, cf. W.O.E. Oesterly and Th.H. Robinson, *Hebrew Religion. Its Origin
and Development*, London 1930 (1952), p. 112, W.B. Barrick, *op. cit.*, pp. 351f.

[134] See, for instance, N. Avigad, "The Governor of the City," *IEJ* 26/76, pp. 178-
182.

[135] Cf. Y. Yadin, "Beer-sheba: The High Place Destroyed by king Josiah," *BASOR*
222/76, pp. 5-18, Barrick, *op. cit.*, pp. 350ff. Y. Shiloh has here misread the Hebrew
text seing the singular העיר as referring to cities, "Iron Age Sanctuaries and Cult
Elements in Palestine," *Symposia*, ed. by F.M. Cross, 1979, p. 152.

because they were שְׂעִירִם [יִ] רִים, "he-goat deities". According to 2 Chr. 11:15, these deities were part of the official cult of the northern kingdom. The question this raises is whether the Beer-Sheba cult place can be seen as an indication that down to the time of king Josiah these gods had been part of — or tolerated by — the official Judahite cult.

In principle a king can, of course, only organize and make changes in territories under his command. His god is the god of the nation and not of people ruled by other kings and their gods. This leads to the problem of how to explain Josiah's actions in the Assyrian province of Samerina, i.e. the former kingdom of Israel. Many scholars have advocated that Josiah's expedition to the north indicates that he annexed this territory to Judah.[136] Unfortunately there is no textual evidence for this. Instead is should be noted that 2 Kings 23:8f. mentions that Josiah's territory streched from Geba in the north to Beer-Sheba in the south. It could, of course, be maintained that this refers to the time before Josiah marched northwards. However, because of the chronistic character of the text one should view the information as referring to Judah's "greatness" under Josiah.

In order to understand both the polemics against Israel in the Old Testament and Josiah's actions in the north, it must be remembered that the official and the national god of Israel was not the Yahweh of Jerusalem. In reality it was the Yahweh of the northern kingdom with its famous shrine at Bethel and its cultic establishment in Samaria. The official religion of the northern kingdom was not at home in or governed from Jerusalem. From a (later) Jerusalemite point of view, Israel was a break-away kingdom, and, thus, both the kingdom and its cult were "wrong."[137] During the time of king Josiah, Bethel was still the most important holy place in the north, carrying on the old traditions of the former nation, cf. 2 Kings 17:28.

From the above it should be evident that Yahweh of Jerusalem had no power over the Assyrian province of Samerina. Josiah's action in this province were more of a hostile nature than anything else. He is said to have burned the temple of Bethel and defiled the altars of the other sanctuaries by massacring the priests and burning their bones on the altars thus making it impossible to use them again. To burn the bones of human beings was considered a punishment, cf. Lev. 20:14, 21:9, Josh. 7:25. In effect, what

---

[136] See, among others, A. Alt, "Judas Gaue unter Josia," *Palästinajahrbuch* 21/25, pp. 100ff. (= *KS* II, pp. 276ff.), M. Noth, *History of Israel,* pp. 273f., J. Bright, *A History of Israel,* 2d ed., 1972, p. 316, S. Herrmann, *A History of Israel in Old Testament Times,* p. 266, A.D. Tushingham, "A Royal Israelite Seal(?) and the Royal Jar Handle Stamps," *BASOR* 201/71, pp. 33ff. F.M. Cross goes so far as to maintain that Josiah "attempted to restore the kingdom or empire of David in all detail," *Canaanite Myth and Hebrew Epic,* p. 283. How can anybody find out anything about Josiah's detailed planning?

[137] This is the basic concept of the book of Amos.

Josiah did was to attempt to stop a rival Yahweh cult over which Jerusalem had neither power nor influence. His expedition to the north was punitive.[138] No text mentions that Josiah reorganized the province as a part of his nation. Indeed, the historian would not have forgotten to record such an event which, had it happened, would have been completely in line with his goals. If Josiah ever contemplated annexing the territory it never came about. His untimely death put an end to any such plan. There is, perhaps, one indication that Josiah tried to extend his territory. If the fortress of Meṣad Ḥashavyahu (Minet Rubin), ca. 1.5 km south of Yavne Yam, was part of Josiah's defense system, as has been maintained, then the king was successful in extending Judah's territory to the west at least.[139]

The Old Testament presentation of the literary phenomenon of the written document, "the law book," found in the temple, 2 Kings 22:8, should be seen as a narrator's construction that conceals the fact that the king himself took the initiative for the reorganization. Indeed, through his temple restoration, he instigated the discovery of the "law book"; he is the one who gave instructions about what steps should be taken.[140] In principle, any king could claim that his god had directed him to take certain actions. As the god's viceroy and administrator, he was the one who revealed the will of his god.[141] Nevertheless, because the narrator of 2 Kings 22 was against any close relationship between god and king that was not mediated by a priest or a prophet, it was necessary to give the reorganization divine authority via a prophetic utterance. This is the role that the prophetess Huldah fills, 2 Kings 22:14ff. In the spirit of the Deuteronomist she is said to have given the king absolution because he humbled himself. Therefore, he will die in peace(!) and not see the disaster that will come over Judah and its capital (the later is certainly a *post eventu* oracle), 22:18ff. This permits the

---

138 See my article, "King Josiah and the DWD of Amos 6:10," *JSS* 26/81, pp. 7-9.

139 For a letter in Hebrew found at this place, see J. Naveh, "A Hebrew Letter from the Seventh Century B.C.," *IEJ* 10/60, pp. 129ff., and "More Hebrew Inscriptions from Meṣad Ḥashavyahu," *IEJ* 12/62, pp. 27ff., A. Lemaire, "L'ostracon de Meṣad Ḥashavyahu (Yavneh-Yam) replacé dans son contexte," *Semitica* 21/71, pp. 57ff., D. Pardee, "An Overview of Ancient Hebrew Epistolography," *JBL* 97/78, pp. 325f. From names such as Obadyahu, Hoshayahu, and Ḥashavyahu it may be concluded that the fortress was under the Judean king. This is, for instance, the opinion of H. Tadmor. He maintains that the Greek pottery found at the place indicates that Josiah had Greek mercenaries in his army, "Philistia under Assyrian Rule," *BA* 29/66, p. 102, n. 59. For the text, see Donner–Röllig, *KAI,* text 200, J.C.L. Gibson, *Textbook of Syrian Semitic Inscriptions* I, pp. 26ff. It could be added that the script seems to be south-Palestinian, not exactly Jerusalemite.

140 Cf. N. Lohfink who points out that everything centers around the king, "Die Bundesurkunde des Königs Josias," *Biblica* 44/63, p. 276.

141 For the king as the "Offenbarungsbringer auf dem Thron," see G. Widengren, *Religionsphänomenologie,* Berlin 1969, pp. 546ff.

assumption that Josiah had already begun some cultic and administrative reforms.

Contentwise the "law book" seems to have been a scroll containing divine commands. In other words, the will of the deity was revealed through these writings.[142] A. Bertholet maintained that the phrase "I have found the law book in the temple of Yahweh," 2 Kings 22:8,[143] is a formula used to give the highest authority to an undertaking. He points to the Egyptian parallel of a newly written text found at the feet of the god Thot in his temple at Hermopolis. The text acquired the character of divine revelation.[144] S. Morenz pointed out that in instances like this one the writing was usually given an archaic character.[145]

As to the authenticity of the "law book", the opinions of A.R. Siebens should be noted. He states that nowhere in the textual material are there any hints that the temple was in such a deplorable state of repair that it needed to be renovated at that point in time.[146] Further, he opines that even if a "book" containing religious laws disappeared, it is certainly strange that its content and main tendencies were forgotten, especially those dealing with cultic rules and practices.[147] Priests usually learned that type of material by rote since it was impractical to carry a *manuale* while sacrificing or while bearing cult symbols in a festival procession. This indicates that if there ever had been such law book which had disappeared, it would not have been difficult to reproduce it.[148]

Sieben's arguments are valid. He seems to have grasped the reality behind the story. It is highly probable, therefore, that Josiah's so called law book was a product of his own time and probably also of his own chancellery, a book made in order to give the king divine authorization for his reorganization program. The narrator used it to suit his own "historiographic" pattern.

Very little is known about the administration of the kings who followed

---

[142] For the divine will being revealed in form of a "book" often "hidden" and "found", see G. Widengren, *op. cit.*, pp. 553f.

[143] One could suspect that the phrase ספר התורה is post-exilic and, as such, a technical term which the narrator has intentionally used in order to see the ideal of the post-exilic community being established already in the pre-exilic time.

[144] *Die Macht der Schrift in Glauben und Aberglauben,* Berlin 1949, pp. 42f., cf. Widengren, *op. cit.,* pp. 553f.

[145] *Ägyptische Religion,* Stuttgart 1960, pp. 231f.

[146] *L'origine du code deuteronomique,* Paris 1929, p. 92.

[147] *Op. cit.,* p. 95.

[148] The religious and social reforms of the early Roman king Numa are interesting parallels. About five hundred years after Numa the praetor Q. Petilius was presented with several books which had been dug up and which were said to be the works of Numa. As a matter of fact, the Roman religious law is said to be based on the *commentarii* (memoranda, writings, proceedings) of Numa, see Edna M. Hooker, "The Significance of Numa's Religious Reform," *Numen* 10/63, pp. 87-132, G. Widengren, *Religionsphänomenologie,* pp. 554f.

Josiah. After his death the situation may have changed and the religious life may have returned to its old forms. This can be concluded from the statements made about Josiah's two sons, Jehoahaz and Jehoiakim. The narrator's evaluation of these two kings is negative. They did what was "evil" in the eyes of Yahweh, exactly as their forefathers had done, 2 Kings 23:32, 37, 24:19. In reality this means that they did not embrace the ideology or follow the customs that the narrator was in favor of, namely the reforms of Hezekiah and Josiah.[149]

---

[149] Cf. Jer. 11:9-13, 32:30ff., Ezek. 8:1ff., 2 Chr. 36:14, and see, among others, J. Pedersen, *Israel* III-IV, p. 295, J. Lindblom, *Prophecy in Ancient Israel*, p. 375, A. Alt, *Kleine Schriften* II, p. 300, V. Maag, "Erwägungen zur deuteronomischen Kultzentralisation," *VT* 6/56, p. 18, E.W. Nicholson, *Deuteronomy and Tradition,* pp. 87ff., G.W. Ahlström, *Joel and the Temple Cult of Jerusalem* (SVT XXI), Leiden 1971, p. 77, n. 3, W. Zimmerli, *Ezechiel* (BK XIII:1), p. 151.

CHAPTER FIVE

KING MANASSEH AND THE REVIVAL OF THE
TRADITIONAL RELIGION OF JUDAH*

Special attention should be paid to the information given in 2 Chr. 33:
14-17, a good example of royal activities concerning the organization of a
nation and its religion. From this passage, as well as from most of the
biblical traditions about the Manasseh regime, we learn that king Manasseh
does not rate very highly in the eyes of the narrators, cf. 2 Kings 21:2,
2 Chr. 33:2. As a matter of fact, he is said to have done more evil than most
others, 2 Kings 21:11ff. and 2 Chr. 33:1ff. Taking into account the religious zeal of the narrators and their goals, it is not astonishing that Manasseh is pictured as one of the worst kings of Judah. What is remarkable,
though, is that most modern scholars have uncritically accepted as historical
the biblical opinion about Manasseh. Consequently, they accuse him of
introducing foreign gods and religious phenomena into Judah and of inaug-
urating a period of rampant syncretism.[1] It is a misleading picture, to say
the least.

A more realistic portrayal of Manasseh can be found through an analysis
of 2 Chr. 33:14-17. This passage states that he was imprisoned for a time in
Babylon.[2] Upon his release and subsequent return to Jerusalem, he fortified

---

* The content of this chapter has been presented in a somewhat different and
abbreviated form in Swedish ("Kung Manasse, en religiös traditionalist") in *Religion
och Bibel* 38, 1979, pp. 9-11.

[1] See, for example, Y. Kaufman, *The Religion of Israel*, Chicago 1960, p. 89,
H. Ringgren, *Israelite Religion*, Philadelphia 1966, p. 276, J. Bright, *A History of
Israel*, 2nd ed., Philadelphia 1972, p. 291, M. Cogan, *Imperialism and Religion*, pp.
88ff., B. Oded, "Judah and the Exile," in *Israelite and Judean History*, ed. by J.H.
Hayes and J.M. Miller, London 1977, p. 453, P.D. Hanson, "Prolegomena to the Study
of Jewish Apocalyptic," in *Magnalia Dei*, p. 398, M. Haran, *Temples and Temple-Service in Ancient Israel*, Oxford 1978, pp. 106f., 278ff., R.M. Seltzer, *Jewish People,
Jewish Thought. The Jewish Experience in History*, New York and London 1980,
p. 103. R.K. Harrison, for instance, writes that during the time of Manasseh "the
people of Judah sank to new depths of depravity and moral degradation," *Old Testament Times*, Grand Rapids, Michigan, 1970, p. 238. The sources, however, do not
verify such a statement. Harrison mistakenly identified cult polemics with the actual
level of popular ethics and morals, something that the texts do not analyze. The narrators are more concerned with the king's doings than with describing the morals of
the population of Judah.

[2] W. Rudolph believes that Manasseh rebelled against Ashurbanipal in connection
with the uprising of Shamash-shum-ukin of Babylon which occurred during the years
652–648 B.C., *Chronikbücher* (HAT 21), Tübingen 1955, pp. 316f. He is followed by

the capital and put "commanders of the army in all fortified cities of Judah." The Chronicler adds that he "took away the foreign gods" and the idol, סמל [3] (a Judahite god image),[4] from the Solomonic temple, and he removed all the altars Solomon had built "on the mountain of the temple of Yahweh and in Jerusalem," v. 15. Although the Chronicler complains that the people were still sacrificing in the sanctuaries, bāmôt, of the country, he adds the qualifier that they now only worshipped Yahweh there.

From this report, which cannot be a complete invention,[5] it is evident not only that Manasseh rebuilt and strengthened his defenses, but that he

---

E. Ehrlich, "Der Aufenthalt des Königs Manasse in Babylon," *ThZ* 21/65, pp. 281ff. See also M. Elat, who refers to the striking parallel of Ashurbanipal's treatment of the rebellious king Necho of Sais in Egypt, thus maintaining that Manasseh and Necho were probably part of the same uprising and dealt with in the same manner, "The Political Status of the Kingdom of Judah within the Assyrian Empire in the 7th Century B.C.E.," in Y. Aharoni, *Investigations at Lachish: The Sanctuary and the Residency (Lachish V)*, Tel Aviv 1975, pp. 66ff. Cf. also E. Nielsen, "Political Conditions and Cultural Development in Israel and Judah during the Reign of Manasseh," *4th World Congress of Jewish Studies* I, Jerusalem 1967, pp. 103ff. As to Assyria's treatment of vassal kings, see also H.W.F. Saggs, *The Greatness that was Babylon*, p. 242. It should be added that Ehrlich points to the fact that Manasseh's sacrifice of his son has a parallel in Ahaz' sacrifice during a politically dangerous situation, 2 Kings 15:37, 16: 3, Isa. 7:1ff., *ThZ* 21/65, p. 283. It is possible that Manasseh's sacrifice of his son, 2 Kings 21:6, 2 Chr. 33:6, was a *mulk*-sacrifice which was usually performed in situations of grave danger, cf. Mesha of Moab, and the Punic custom of sacrificing children to Tanit and Baal Hammon in politically troubled times. The Jerusalemites seem to have done the same in the *tōphet* in the valley of Hinnom, 2 Kings 23:10, Jer. 7:31, 32:34f., Ezek. 16:20. If Manasseh was threatened by the Assyrians, it is possible that the sacrifice of his son occurred in this connection. With A.T. Olmstead the *mulk*-sacrifices should be viewed as having been directed to Yahweh, *History of Assyria*, Chicago 1923 (1960), p. 379. So also J. Lindblom, *Israels religion i gammaltestamentlig tid*, 2nd ed., Stockholm 1953, p. 155.

[3] The phrase את־פסל הסמל in v. 7 clearly indicates that we are dealing with a statue and not a slab, as W.F. Albright concluded with the help of 8:3,5. By rendering מושב, "niche" instead of seat, place, postament, he was able to place a slab into a niche and thus view the phenomenon as Syro-Assyrian, *Archaeology and the Religion of Israel*, 2nd ed., Baltimore 1946, pp. 165f. It should be noted that the tradition in 2 Kings 21:7 has פסל האשרה. Knowing that Asherah was an Israelite goddess (cf. Ahlström, *Aspects of Syncretism in Israelite Religion*, 1963, pp. 50ff.), the *semel* of 2 Chr. 33:7, 15 *may* be a reference to Asherah. However, this term is never used elsewhere for Asherah's idol. Here we should add that in Dt. 4:16 the word *semel* refers to a deity statue, male or female. It should also be noted that in the Phoenician language of Cyprus *semel* never refers to a statue of a goddess, cf. Z.S. Harris, *A Grammar of the Phoenician Language* (AOS 8), New Haven, Conn., 1936, p. 60, §18:1. For *sml* as referring to a god statue, see also the Azitawadda text from Karatepe, *KAI* 26:IV:14f., and 18f.

[4] H.D. Preuss does not believe that two deity categories are mentioned here, *Verspottung fremder Religionen im Alten Testament* (BWANT 92), Stuttgart 1971, p. 174.

[5] See, for instance, W. Rudolph, *Chronikbücher*, pp. 315f., R. North, "Does Archaeology Prove Chronicles Sources?," *A Light Unto My Path* (Old Testament

carried out a cultic reorganization around the same time. Here one could ask whether a connection exists between strengthening the defense system and reforming or reorganizing cult and administration. Before attempting an answer, it should be noted that Asa (2 Chr. 14:3ff.), Hezekiah, and Josiah also seem to have undertaken a reorganization of the religious system in connection with building activities, defense improvements or in connection with a change in foreign policy.[6] The solution to this question must lie somewhere within the complex idea of religion as a national, territorial phenomenon, for, as we have seen, politics and religion went hand in hand. Therefore, a change in either foreign policy or territorial area demanded consequent changes in military and cultic personnel. When 2 Chr. 33:14ff. mentions that Manasseh sent army commanders to the fortified cities of his kingdom, it does not mean that they did not have any commanders there before. The fact is that the army command had to be changed! This text shows that Manasseh, who had inherited a city state, obviously recovered some, if not all, of the territory that his father, Hezekiah, lost;[7] territory which Sennacherib had added to the Philistine holdings dividing it up between Sillibel of Gaza, Padi of Ekron, and Mitinti of Ashdod.[8] With the

---

Studies in Honor of J.M. Myers), ed. by N.H. Bream, R. Heim, C.A. Moore, Philadelphia 1973, pp. 383ff., B. Oded, "Judah and the Exile," in *Israelite and Juden History*, p. 455. R. Frankena assumes that Manasseh, together with twenty-one other vassal kings, was present as Ashurbanipal's crown prince installation on the 12th of Iyyar 672 B.C. These twenty-two vassal kings are mentioned in the *Annals of Esarhaddon* (Nin. V:55ff.) as having delivered building materials to the Assyrian king. In this text Manasseh is called the *šar* ^{uru}*Ia'ūdi*, "king of (the city of) Judah," see Frankena, "The Vassal Treaties of Esarhaddon and the Dating of Deuteronomy," *Oudtestamentische Studiën* 14/65, pp. 150f. This shows that at this time Judah was still a city state and that, therefore, Manasseh could not have retrieved the Judahite cities prior to that time. Because Manasseh's son and successor bore the Egyptian name Amon, A.T. Olmstead concluded that Manasseh supported Psammeticus I's revolution against Assyria, *History of Assyria*, p. 380. Whatever actually happened, the Assyrian king's act of grace in letting Manasseh continue as king of Judah was turned by the biblical "historian" into an act of grace of Yahweh. History has here been translated into theology.

6 For the "topos" of building activities and cult reorganization, see now P. Welten, *Geschichte und Geschichtsdarstellung in den Chronikbüchern*, 1973, pp. 5f., and pp. 180ff.

7 The Assyrian Annals mention 46 fortified cities and several smaller settlements, cf. A. Alt, *Kleine Schriften* II, pp. 242ff., H.L. Ginsberg, "Judah and the Transjordan States from 734 to 582 B.C.E.," *Alexander Marx Jubilee Volume*, New York 1950, pp. 349ff., C. van Leeuwen, "Sanchérib devant Jerusalem," *Oudtestamentische Studiën* 14/65, p. 246. For the text, see D.D. Luckenbill, *The Annals of Sennacherib* (OIP II), Chicago 1924, pp. 32f., lines 18ff.

8 One of the Akkadian texts mentions besides these three cities also Ashkalon (*ARAB* II §312, Luckenbill, *op. cit.*, p. 70, lines 28-30), cf. H. Tadmor, "Philistia under Assyrian Rule," *BA* 29/66, p. 97.

return of these territories, or a part of them, Philistine rule ended. Therefore, Manasseh's administration had to be extended in order to re-incorporate these cities territorially and religiously into the kingdom of Judah. This was accomplished by sending out Judahite commanders, troops, and civil servants, including priests. Only when the official religion of Judah was established according to its *mišpāṭ* (rule, and norms) could Yahweh's rule be re-established. The sanctuaries, *bāmôt*, of these cities again became sanctuaries of the nation of Judah and its official religion.[9] Therefore, the purpose of both the military and the cultic reorganization that Manasseh undertook was the same: to incorporate the regained territory into his kingdom.[10]

Military defense meant, among other things, repairing existing structures and building new fortifications and walls. For example, Manasseh built an outer wall for Jerusalem encircling the Ophel, "in the west to Gihon (which is) in the valley" and extending to the entrance of the Fish Gate in the north, 2 Chr. 33:14. It not only provided an extra defense wall for the Ophel, but since it seems to have extended west of the original city, it gave added protection for the population of the Western Hill. Although the city's population seems to have increased after the time of king Hezekiah, most of the newcomers could not have moved into the city proper because of lack of space. Thus, the Western Hill became a "suburb" providing a new area of settlement. Archaeological remains support such an hypothesis. For example, M. Broshi maintained that the city of Jerusalem "expanded to three to four times its former size" around 700 B.C.[11] He suggests that the increase was due to immigration from the former kingdom of Israel after its collapse and from former Judahite towns and districts which Sennacherib added to the territory of Philistine kings in 701 B.C.[12] Broshi's hypothesis may provide part of the answer to Jerusalem's growth after 721 B.C. Unfortunately, the idea that people escaped from the captured cities in 701 B.C. is unsubstantiated. Moreover, it is doubtful that the Philistine governments permitted any kind of exodus. These governments were now responsible to the Assyrians for the population put under their supervision. The fact that people settled outside the walls of Jerusalem after 701 B.C. can partly be explained by recalling that the area of Judah in this period was no larger than Jerusalem and its closest surroundings. Those (from the country side?)

---

[9] This may be the reality behind the statement in 2 Chr. 33:17 asserting that the people now worshipped only "Yahweh, their god" at these *bāmôt*.

[10] Compare also the cult organization undertaken by Jeroboam I who had to organize a new kingdom, and, thus, also its cult.

[11] This may be an exaggeration.

[12] "The Expansion of Jerusalem in the Reign of Hezekiah and Manasseh," *IEJ* 24/74, pp. 21-26. For a discussion about Manasseh's wall, see also J. Simons, "The Wall of Manasseh and the 'Mishneh'," *Oudtestamentische Studiën* 7/50, pp. 179ff., Th. A. Busink, *Der Tempel von Jerusalem* I, pp. 102f.

who escaped the war may have settled close to the city of Jerusalem, thus remaining subjects of the king of Judah. This may then be the beginning of the *mishneh,* "the second city," that is mentioned in 2 Kings 22:14 and in Zech. 1:10.

It is possible that Manasseh's wall joined up with the one that his father, Hezekiah, had built outside, לחוצה, the old city wall, 2 Chr. 32:5. Hezekiah's wall may be the great wall (up to 7 m wide) that was unearthed on the Western Hill in the Jewish Quarter of the Old City of modern Jerusalem.[13] It is conceivable that this wall encircled the above mentioned suburb, the *mishneh.*[14] Thus the Jerusalem of Hezekiah's time may have been a double city (cf. the dual form *"Y^erūšalayim"*). If Manasseh's wall was connected with this wall of Hezekiah it would have made the city one again.

Of other fortifications associated with king Manasseh the so-called Manasseh wall on the acropolis of Tell el-Ḥesi should be mentioned. This is an identification made by F. Petrie.[15] If this is correct, Ḥesi (Eglon?) may have been one of the cities Manasseh retrieved. The defense activities of this king may very well have been directed against Egypt.[16] Having become a faithful Assyrian vassal his building activities may be seen as a result of this policy.

In making Manasseh the scape goat for the disaster of the country, the Chronicler appears as an exponent of the ancient Near Eastern concept whereby a deity's displeasure with his people forces him to destroy the nation.[17] It must be asked, however, why the blame was placed on Manasseh,

---

[13] N. Avigad, "Excavations in the Jewish Quarter of the Old City of Jerusalem 1969/1970," *IEJ* 20/70, pp. 1ff., 129ff., and *IEJ* 22/72, pp. 193ff. – The Fish Gate was located in the north. Therefore, Manasseh's wall seems to have streched from the west to Gihon in the Kedron valley encircling the Ophel. Unfortunately we do not know where in the west it started. Consequently, the connection with Hezekiah's wall remains hypothetical.

[14] This has been discussed in my review of K.M. Kenyon's book *Digging up Jerusalem* in the *Journal of Near Eastern Studies* 37/78, pp. 65f. In this review I expressed the opinion that the wall did not encircle a settlement to the south and that it was not connected with the already existing wall of Jerusalem. This seems now to have been supported by A.D. Tushingham, "The Western Hill (of Jerusalem) under the Monarchy," *ZDPV* 95/79, pp. 39-55. For the "Broad Wall" of Nehemiah 3:8, see R. Grafman, "Nehemiah's 'Broad Wall'," *IEJ* 24/74, pp. 50f., G.W. Ahlström, *Joel and the Temple Cult of Jerusalem,* p. 115.

[15] *Tell el Ḥesy (Lachish),* London 1891, pp. 32f., and plates II, III. See also K.G. O'Connell, D.G. Rose, L.E. Toombs, "Tell el-Hesi," *IEJ* 27/77, p. 248.

[16] Cf. E. Sellin, *Geschichte des israelitisch-jüdischen Volkes* I, 1924, p. 281. Here one could ask whether the fortress of Arad and the surrounding area had been returned to Manasseh or was it first taken back by Josiah? Did the the Philistines, or Manasseh, or Josiah build stratum VII?

[17] Cf. S.N. Kramer, "Lamentation over the Destruction of Sumer and Ur," *The Ancient Near East* (Suppl. to ANET), ed. by J.B. Pritchard, Princeton 1969, pp. 175ff. (611 ff.). Consult also B. Albrektson, *History and the Gods* (Coniectanea Biblica, OT Series 1), Lund 1967, pp. 27ff.

who, after all, "converted" to Yahweh, according to the Chronicler, 2 Chr. 33:12-13. Indeed, one may ask why the blame was not levelled against Jehoiakim or Zedekiah.

We can attribute the unflattering evaluation of Manasseh given by the narrators of 2 Kings and 2 Chronicles to the fact that he abandoned the policies of his father, Hezekiah, a king whose works harmonized well with the narrator's own theology. According to the standards of their time, Hezekiah's reform was the ideal against which the religious customs of the pre-exilic era were to be evaluated. In Manasseh's eyes, however, the policies of Hezekiah had led the country to the brink of disaster. Therefore, Manasseh's cultic reform may have been nothing more than a return to the religious situation that existed before Hezekiah's innovations. 2 Kings 21:3 may, thus, be the narrator's personal view of Manasseh's cultic restoration program.[18] If the above interpretation is correct, Manasseh cannot be called an "apostate", as may scholars prefer to label him.[19] He was rather a traditionalist in religious matters, and as such he came into conflict with those groups still advocating the religious ideas and the radical, utopian innovations of his "unorthodox" father. Therefore, Manasseh had to neutralize those elements;[20] they may be seen as enemies of the state.

This example from Manasseh's reign shows how intimately interwoven religion and state were. The king, as head of state, was also the head of the national religion as his god's viceroy.[21] Fortress cities, fortresses, store cities

---

[18] B. Oded assumes that Manasseh "seems to have intended the creation of a genuine syncretism of Yahwistic and pagan cults," in *Israelite and Judean History*, p. 453. This is, however, more conjecture than history because it is unknown whether Manasseh had any such intentions. Oded builds solely upon the Chronicler's theological construction and his hatred for Manasseh. What we know is that the narrator liked to put his own Yahwistic ideals into the time of Manasseh and use them as a yardstick for his evaluations of the king. Thus, he blames Manasseh for the old Judahite religious phenomena he did not like. B. Peckham's suggestion that the "sanctuary" from ca. 700 B.C. found in the excavations by K.M. Kenyon in Jerusalem (see *Digging up Jerusalem*, p. 143) was a "representative of the Phoenician cults introduced by Manasseh" ("Israel and Phoenicia," in *Magnalia Dei*, p. 238) is nothing more than a guess. We do not even know whether this building was a sanctuary.

[19] From a methodological viewpoint the term apostate should not be used because it is a subjective evaluation, cf. Morton Smith, "The Veracity of Ezekiel, the Sins of Manasseh, and Jeremiah 44:18," *ZAW* 87/75, p. 12. W.F. Stinespring's negative verdict about Manasseh's religious actions is nothing more than an uncritical acceptance of the Chronicler's evaluation, "Temple, Jerusalem," *IDB* IV, p. 539. He is followed by, among others, P.D. Hanson, "Prolegomena to the Study of Jewish Apocalyptic," in *Magnalia Dei*, p. 398.

[20] Cf. Morton Smith, *Palestinian Parties and Politics that Shaped the Old Testament*, New York and London 1971, p. 40.

[21] Texts such as these about king Manasseh, as well as others which sharply criticize the kings, cannot possibly have been written or made public during the time of the

and royal sanctuaries were the visible arms of the central government in its administration of the different areas of the nation, all of which comprised the territory of the nation's god.

---

monarchy. That would have been understood as hostility toward the state, and, as such, close to treason. Thus, they most probably belong to a period when there was no Judahite king who could sentence the writers. Finally, concerning the History of Israel and Judah one could apply the following quote from E. H. Carr: "Our picture has been preselected and predetermined for us, not so much by accident as by people who were consciously imbued with a particular view, and thought the facts, which supported that view worth preserving." *What is History?,* London 1961, p. 13.

APPENDIX

It has been advocated on textual grounds, that sanctuaries called *bāmôt* existed in many, if not most, of the Israelite and Judahite cities. That so few of these sanctuaries from the monarchic time have been uncovered during excavations in Palestine may be due to the fact that a tell is seldom completely excavated and many have not been dug at all. Moreover, some buildings may have been incorrectly identified. The number of sanctuaries may, however, be increased if the so-called bench-rooms found at Tell ed-Duweir and Kuntillet 'Ajrud are taken into account, and there may have been more of this kind. Such a conclusion could also be drawn from 2 Kings 23:8. Indeed, a cult room may have existed inside the entrance of a fortress or in close connection with a city gate. In this connection the structure in the gate of Israelite Dan is illustrative. It has been identified as a "base for a throne" or for an idol.[1] Perhaps this place served the dual purpose of cult room and meeting place for the elders of the city, a place where both religious and civil duties were performed. Offerings and tithes were deposited in the bench-rooms where government officials called Levites may have collected and accounted for them. Thus, separate sanctuary buildings were not necessary everywhere. Whether these cult rooms were put out of business with the reform of king Josiah is impossible to determine. Taking into consideration the fact that tithes had to be collected throughout the country one may conclude that these bench-rooms still fulfilled a purpose.[2]

One more observation about the religious situation must be made. If one considers all the human and animal figurines that have been found in the soil of Iron Age Palestine, one is struck by the great amount found in Jerusalem as compared with other sites. Thus far Jerusalem has contributed (up to 1975) a total of 597 figurines. These include 149 "pillar" figurines, 119 horse and rider figurines, and 258 animal figurines. Samaria has a total of 159 (39-25-21), Bethel (Beitin) 28 (7-2-10), Dan accounts for only one (a "pillar" figurine), Shechem 22 (4-1-3), Gibeon 64 (27-13-15), Hazor 44 (7-3-5).[3] Jerusalem's religious attachment to the symbols of horses,

---

[1] A. Biran, "Tel Dan," *BA* 37/74, pp. 45, 47. For a possible "cult-installation" inside the gate of Area K (LB II) at Hazor, see Y. Yadin, *Hazor,* London 1972, p. 63.

[2] Because of the gods worshipped at the cult place inside the gate mentioned in 2 Kings 23:8 it was destroyed by king Josiah. Thus, it must be considered a special case.

[3] See the statistics in T.A. Holland, "A Study of Palestinian Iron Age Baked Clay Figurines, with Special Reference to Jerusalem: Cave 1," *Levant* 9/77, pp. 121ff. Concerning the figurines found in Jerusalem it should be noted that Cave 1 (on the eastern

bulls and nude women seems to be quite pronounced and must be considered in any treatment of the religions of Israel and Judah. The bull figurines, for example, are much more common in Jerusalem than in any other place. Recalling the polemics against the bull worship of the kingdom of Israel found in both historical and prophetical books, one can only conclude that the picture drawn for us of the northern kingdom and its religion is not reliable. Furthermore, the so-called conservative Yahwism which is said to have predominated in Judah,[4] seems to have existed only in the biblical writers' reconstruction of the history. It would certainly be an overstatement to maintain that all the figurines must be viewed as popular religious phenomena that have no connection with the official religion of the nation.[5] We know too little about the actual rituals of any cult place including those of the Solomonic temple, and our knowledge of the beliefs and customs of the common man is scant. Thus, comparison of "popular" religion and the national religion is almost impossible.

---

slope) contained ca. 1300 objects of which only 84 were animal or human figurines. This fact can, of course, not be used to argue that the area was sacred, because such figurines have been found in several other places in Jerusalem.

[4] J. Bright, for instance, assumed that the Jerusalem priests usually came down "on the side of conservatism where religious matters were concerned," *A History of Israel*, 2nd ed., p. 235. One could, of course, ask what kind of conservatism is meant.

[5] In this connection one should realize that a large number of the inhabitants of Jerusalem, a capital, were probably government employees. As such they were representatives of the nation's political and religious system.

BIBLIOGRAPHY

Abel, F.M., *Géographie de la Palestine* II, Paris 1938.

Ackroyd, P.R., "The Age of the Chronicler" (The Selwyn Lectures for 1970 delivered at the College of Saint John the Evangelist, Auckland, New Zealand), *Colloquium* 1970, pp. 5-60.

——, *The First Book of Samuel* (The Cambridge Bible Commentary, New English Bible), Cambridge 1971.

——, "History and Theology in the Writings of the Chronicler," *Concordia Theological Monthly* 38, 1967, pp. 501-515.

Adams, R.M., see Kraeling, C.H.

Aharoni, Y., "Arad: Its Inscriptions and Temple," *BA* 31, 1968, pp. 2-32.

——, *Arad Inscriptions* (Judean Desert Series), Jerusalem 1975.

——, "Tel Beer-sheba," *IEJ* 24, 1974, pp. 270-272.

——, "Tel Beer-sheba, 1975," *IEJ* 25, 1975, pp. 169-171.

——, "Forerunners of the Limes: Iron Age Fortresses in the Negev," *IEJ* 17, 1967, pp. 1-17.

——, "The Horned Altar of Beer-sheba," *BA* 37, 1974, pp. 2-6.

——, *Investigations at Lachish. The Sanctuary and the Residency (Lachish V)*, Tel Aviv, 1975.

——, "Lachish," *IEJ* 18, 1968, pp. 254-255.

——, *The Land of the Bible*, Philadelphia 1967.

——, "The Negeb," in *Archaeology and the Old Testament Study*, ed. by D.W. Thomas, Oxford 1967, pp. 385-403.

——, "Nothing Early and Nothing Late: Rewriting Israel's Conquest," *BA* 39, 1976, pp. 55-76.

——, "The Province-List of Judah," *VT* 9, 1959, pp. 225-246.

——, "Seals of Royal Functionaries from Arad," *Eretz Israel* 8, 1967, pp. 101-103 (Hebrew).

——, "The Solomonic Temple, the Tabernacle and the Arad Sanctuary," *Orient and Occident* (AOAT 22), 1973, pp. 1-8.

——, "Trial Excavation in the 'Solar Shrine' at Lachish. Preliminary Report," *IEJ* 18, 1968, pp. 159-169.

——, "The Use of Hieratic Numerals in Hebrew Ostraca and the Shekel Weights," *BASOR* 184, 1966, pp. 13-19.

——, (ed.), *Beer-Sheba I. Excavations at Tel Beer-Sheba, 1969–1971 Seasons* (Tel Aviv University, Publications of the Institute of Archaeology 2), Tel Aviv 1973.

Aharoni, Y. and Amiran, R., "A New Scheme for the Sub-Division of the Iron Age in Palestine," *IEJ* 8, 1958, pp. 171-184.

Aharoni, Y., Fritz, V., and Kempinski, A., "Vorbericht über die Ausgrabungen auf der Hirbet el-Mšāš (Tel Māšôš), 1. Kampagne 1972," *ZDPV* 89, 1973, pp. 197-210.

——, "Excavations at Tel Masos (Khirbet el-Meshâsh). Preliminary Report on the First Season, 1972," *Tel Aviv* 1, 1974, pp. 64-74.

Ahlström, G.W., "Another Moses Tradition," *JNES* 39, 1980, pp. 65-69.

——, *Aspects of Syncretism in Israelite Religion*, Lund 1963.

——, "Heaven on Earth – at Hazor and Arad," *Religious Syncretism in Antiquity*, ed. by B.A. Pearson, Missoula, Mont., 1975, pp. 67-83.

——, "Is Tell ed-Duweir Ancient Lachish?", *PEQ* 112, 1980, pp. 7-9.

——, *Joel and the Temple Cult of Jerusalem* (SVT 21), Leiden 1971.

——, "King Jehu – A Prophet's Mistake," in *Scripture in History and Theology. Essays in Honor of J.C. Rylaarsdam*, ed. by A.L. Merrill and T.W. Overholt, Pittsburg 1977, pp. 47-69.

——, "King Josiah and the DWD of Amos 6:10," *JSS* 26, 1981, pp. 7-9.

——, "Notes to Isaiah 53:8f," *BZ* 13, 1969, pp. 95-98.

——, "Prophecy," *Encyclopaedia Britannica* 15, 15th ed., Chicago 1974, pp. 62-68.

——, "Der Prophet Nathan und der Tempelbau," *VT* 11, 1961, pp. 113-127.

——, *Psalm 89*, Lund 1959.

——, "Solomon, the Chosen One," *History of Religions* 8, 1968, pp. 93-110.

——, "Was David a Jebusite Subject?" *ZAW* 92, 1980, pp. 285-287.

——, "Winepresses and Cup-Marks of the Jenin–Megiddo Survey," *BASOR* 231, 1978, pp. 19-49.

——, Rev. of K.M. Kenyon, Digging up Jerusalem, *JNES* 37, 1978, pp. 62-67.

Albrektson, B., *History and the Gods. An Essay on the Idea of Historical Events as Divine Manifestations in the Ancient Near East and in Israel* (Coniectanea Biblica. Old Testament Series 1), Lund 1967.

Albright, W.F., "Akkadian Letters," in *ANET*, pp. 482-490.

——, *Archaeology and the Religion of Israel*, 2nd ed., Baltimore 1946.

——, "*The Excavation of Tell Beit Mirsim, III: The Iron Age* (AASOR 21-22), New Haven 1943.

——, "New Canaanite Historical and Mythological Data," *BASOR* 63, 1936, pp. 23-32.

——, "Cuneiform Material for Egyptian Prosopography 1500–1200 B.C.," *JNES* 5, 1946, pp. 7-25.

——, "The Judicial Reform of Jehoshphat," *Alexander Marx Jubilee Volume*, New York 1950, pp. 61-82.

——, "The List of Levitic Cities," *L. Ginsberg Jubilee Volume*, New York 1945, pp. 49-74.

——, "A Prince of Taanach in the Fifteenth Century B.C.," *BASOR* 94, 1944, pp. 12-27.

Albright, W.F. and Kelso, J.L., *The Excavation of Bethel (1934–1960)* (AASOR 39), Cambridge, Mass., 1968.

Allan, N., "Jeroboam and Shechem," *VT* 24, 1974, pp. 353-357.

Alster, B., "Early Patterns in Mesopotamian Literature," *Kramer Anniversary Volume* (AOAT 25), 1976, pp. 13-24.

Alt, A., "Ägyptische Tempel in Palästina und die Landnahme der Philister," *ZDPV* 67, 1944, pp. 1-20 (*KS* I, München 1953, pp. 216-230).

——, "Bemerkungen zu einigen jüdäischen Ortslisten des Alten Testaments," *Beiträge zur biblischen Landes- und Altertumskunde* 68, 1951, pp. 193-210 (*KS* II, München 1953, pp. 289-305).

——, "Festungen und Levitenorte im Lande Juda," *KS* II, München 1953, pp. 306-315.

——, "The Formation of the Israelite State in Palestine," *Essays in Old Testament History and Religion*, Garden City, N.Y., 1967, pp. 223-309.

——, "Zur Geschichte von Beth-Shan," *Palästinajahrbuch* 22, 1926, pp. 108-120 (*KS* I, München 1953, pp. 246-255).

——, "Judas Gaue unter Josia," *Palästinajahrbuch* 21, 1925, pp. 100-116 (*KS* II, München 1953, pp. 276-288).

——, "Neues über Palästina aus dem Archiv Amenophis IV," *Palästinajahrbuch* 20, 1924, pp. 22-41 (*KS* III, München 1959, pp. 169-175).

——, "The Settlement of the Israelites in Palestine," *Essays in Old Testament History and Religion,* Garden City, N.Y., 1967, pp. 173-221.

——, "Die Stadtstaat Samaria," *KS* III, München 1959, pp. 258-302.

——, "Das System der Assyrischen Provinzen auf dem Boden des Reiches Israel," *ZDPV* 52, 1929, pp. 220-242 (*KS* II, München 1953, pp. 188-205).

——, "Die territorialgeschichtliche Bedeutung von Sanheribs Eingriff in Palästina," *Palästinajahrbuch* 25, 1930, pp. 80-88 (*KS* II, München 1953, pp. 242-249).

Amiran, R., see Aharoni, Y.

Anderson, F.I., "Moabite Syntax," *Orientalia* N.S. 35, 1966, pp. 81-119.

Ap-Thomas, D.R., "All the King's Horses," in *Proclamation and Presence,* ed. by J.I. Durham and J.R. Porter, Richmond, Virginia, 1970, pp. 135-151.

——, "Saul's Uncle," *VT* 11, 1961, pp. 241-245.

Auerbach, E., "Der Aufstieg der Priesterschaft zur Macht im Alten Israel," *SVT* 9, 1963, pp. 236-247.

——, "Die Herkunft der Sadokiden," *ZAW* 49, 1931, pp. 327-328.

Auld, A.G., "The 'Levitical Cities': Text and History," *ZAW* 91, 1979, pp. 194-206.

Avigad, N., "Excavations in the Jewish Quarter of the Old City of Jerusalem 1969/ 1970," *IEJ* 20, 1970, pp. 129-140.

——, "Excavations in the Jewish Quarter of the Old City of Jerusalem, 1971," *IEJ* 22, 1972, pp. 193-200.

——, "The Governor of the City," *IEJ* 26, 1976, pp. 178-182.

——, "The Priest of Dor," *IEJ* 25, 1975, pp. 101-105.

Badaway, A., "The Civic Sense of Pharaoh and Urban Development in Ancient Egypt," *Journal of the American Research Center in Egypt* 6, 1967, pp. 103-109.

Barnett, R.D., see Wolley, L.

Barrick, W.B., *The World BMH in the Old Testament* (Unpubl. Ph.D. dissertation, University of Chicago), Chicago 1977.

Barrois, A.-G., *Manuel d'archéologie biblique* II, Paris 1953.

Bechtel, G., see Sturtevant, E.H.

Begrich, J., "Sōphēr und Mazkīr. Ein Beitrag zur inneren Geschichte des davidisch-salomonischen Grossreiches und des Königreiches Juda," *ZAW* 58, 1940–41, pp. 1-29.

Ben-Dov, M., "נפה – Geographical Term of Possible 'Sea People' Origin," *Tel Aviv* 3, 1976, pp. 70-73.

Bennett, C.-M., "Excavations at Buseirah, Southern Jordan 1972: Preliminary Report," *Levant* 6, 1974, pp. 1-24.

Bentzen, Aa., "The Cultic Use of the Story of the Ark in Samuel," *JBL* 67, 1948, pp. 37-53.

——, *Studier over det sadokidiske Praesteskabs Historie,* København 1931.

Bernhardt, K.-H., *Die Umwelt des Alten Testaments* I, 2nd ed., Berlin 1968.

——, "Verwaltungspraxis im spätbronzezeitlichen Palästina," *Beitrag zur sozialen Struktur des Alten Vorderasien* (Schriften zur Geschichte und Kultur des Alten Orient I), ed. by H. Klengel, Berlin 1971, pp. 133-147.

Bertholet, A., *Die Macht der Schrift in Glauben und Aberglauben,* Berlin 1949.

Bezold, C. and A., and Goetze, A., *Babylonisch-assyrisches Glossar,* Heilderberg 1926.

Biran, A., "Tel Dan," *BA* 37, 1974, pp. 26-51.

Biran, A., see Mazar, B.

Birch, B.C., *The Rise of the Israelite Monarchy: The Growth and Development of I Samuel 7-15* (SBL Dissertation Series 27), Missoula, Mont., 1976.

Birot, M., *Lettres de Yaqqim-Addu, gouverneur de Sagaratum* (ARM XIV), Paris 1974.

Black, M., "The Zakir Stele," in *Documents from Old Testament Times,* ed. by D.W. Thomas, London 1958, pp. 242-250.

Blenkinsopp, J., *Gibeon and Israel* (Society for Old Testament Study 2), Cambridge 1972.

Bliss, F.J. and Macalister, R.A.S., *Excavations in Palestine during the years 1898–1900*, London 1902.

Boling, R.G., *Judges* (Anchor Bible 6A), Garden City, N.Y., 1975.

Boraas, R.S. and Geraty, L.T., "The Fourth Campaign at Tell Ḥesbân," *Andrews University Seminary Studies* 14, 1976, pp. 1-16.

Borée, W., *Die alte Ortsnamen Palästinas*, Hildesheim 1968.

Borger, R., *Die Inschriften Asarhaddons, Königs von Assyrien*, Graz 1956.

Branden, A. van den, *Les inscriptions Dédanite*, Beirut 1962.

Bright, J., *A History of Israel*, 2nd ed., Philadelphia 1972.

Brockelmann, C., *Hebräische Syntax*, Neukirchen 1956.

Broshi, M., "The Expansion of Jerusalem in the Reign of Hezekiah and Manasseh," *IEJ* 24, 1974, pp. 21-26.

Brown, J.P., "The Sacrificial Cult and its Critique in Greek and Hebrew (I)," *JSS* 24, 1979, pp. 159-173.

Buccellati, G., *The Amorites in the Ur III Period* (Publicazioni del Seminario di Semitistica, Ricerche I), Naples 1966.

——, *Cities and Nations of Ancient Syria* (Studi Semitici 26), Rome 1967.

Budde, K., *Die altisraelitische Religion*, Giessen 1912.

Burney, C.F., *The Book of Judges*, London 1918.

Busink Th.A., *Der Tempel von Jerusalem* I, Leiden 1970.

Butto, B.F., *Studies on Women at Mari* (The Johns Hopkins Near Eastern Studies), Baltimore 1974.

Butz, K., "Konzentrationen wirtschaftlicher Macht im Königreich Larsa: Der Nanna-Ningal Tempelkomplex in Ur," *Wiener Zeitschrift für die Kunde des Morgenlandes* 65/66, 1973-74, pp. 1-58.

Canciani, F. and Pettinato, G., "Salomos Thron, philologische und archäologische Erwägungen," *ZDPV* 81, 1965, pp. 88-108.

Carlson, R.A., *David, the Chosen King*, Stockholm–Uppsala–Göteborg 1964.

——, "Profeten Amos och Davidsriket," *Religion och Bibel* 25, 1966, pp. 57-78.

Carr, E.H., *What is History?*, London 1961.

Claburn, W.E., "The Fiscal Basis of Josiah's Reforms," *JBL* 92, 1973, pp. 11-22.

Clark, W.M., *The Origin and Development of the Land Promise Theme in the Old Testament* (Unpubl. Ph.D. dissertation, Yale University), New Haven 1964.

Clarke, S., "Ancient Egyptian Frontier Fortresses," *JEA* 3, 1916, pp. 155-179.

Clements, R.E., "The Deuteronomistic Interpretation of the Founding of the Monarchy in I Sam. VIII," *VT* 24, 1974, pp. 398-410.

Cody, A., *A History of the Old Testament Priesthood* (Analecta Biblica 35), Rome 1969.

——, "When is the Chosen People called a *gôy*?," *VT* 14, 1964, pp. 1-6.

——, "Le titre égyptien et le nom propre du scribe de David," *RB* 72, 1965, pp. 381-393.

Cogan, M., *Imperialism and Religion: Assyria, Judah and Israel in the Eighth and Seventh Centuries B.C.E.*, Missoula, Mont, 1974.

Cohen, M.A., "In All Fairness to Ahab – A Socio-Political Consideration of the Ahab – Elijah Conflict," *Eretz Israel* 12, 1975, pp. 87*-94*.

Condon, V., *Seven Royal Hymns of the Ramesside Period, Papyrus Turin CG54031* (Münchener Ägyptologische Studien 37), München 1978.

Cross, F.M., *Canaanite Myth and Hebrew Epic*, Cambridge, Mass., 1973.

——, "The History of the Biblical Text in Light of Discoveries in the Judean Desert," *HTR* 57, 1964, pp. 281-299.

Crowfoot, G.M., see Crowfoot, J.W.

Crowfoot, J.W., Crowfoot, G.M., and Kenyon, K.M., *Samaria-Sebaste III: The Objects from Samaria,* London 1957.

Crown, A., "Some Factors Relating to Settlement and Urbanization in Ancient Canaan in the Second and First Millennia B.C.," *Abr-Nahrain* 11, 1971, pp. 22-41.

Dahood, M., "Hebrew-Ugaritic Lexicography V," *Biblica* 48, 1967, pp. 421-438.

Davies, A.M., see Hawkins, J.O.

Deimel, A., *Sumerische Tempelwirtschaft* (Analecta Orientalia 2), Rome 1931.

Delekat, L., "Zum hebräischen Wörterbuch," *VT* 14, 1964, pp. 7-66.

Demsky, A., "Geba, Gibeah, and Gibeon – an Historico-geographical Riddle," *BASOR* 212, 1973, pp. 26-31.

Dhorme, E., *L'évolution religieuse d'Israël,* Brussels 1937.

Dimbleby, G.W., see Ucko, P.J.

Diringer, D., *Le iscrizioni antico-ebraiche palestinesi,* Firenze 1934.

Donner, H., "Der 'Freund des Königs'," *ZAW* 73, 1961, pp. 269-277.

——, "The Separate States of Israel and Judah," in *Israelite and Judean History,* ed. by J.H. Hayes and J.M. Miller, Philadelphia 1977, pp. 381-434.

Donner, H. and Röllig, W., *Kanaanäische und Aramäische Inschriften* I-III, Wiesbaden 1962–64.

Dossin, G., "Le panthéon de Mari," *Studia Mariana,* ed. by A. Parrot, Leiden 1950, pp. 41-50.

Dothan, M., see Mazar, B.

Dougherty, R.P., "Cuneiform Parallels to Solomon's Provisioning System," *AASOR* 5, 1923–24, pp. 23-65.

Driver, S.R., *Notes on the Hebrew Text to the Books of Samuel,* Oxford 1890.

Dunayevsky, I., see Mazar, B.

Ebeling, E., see Knudtzon, J.A.

Edel, E., *Die Ortsnamenlisten aus dem Totentempel Amenophis III* (Bonner Biblische Beiträge 25), Bonn, 1966.

Edelstein, G., see Levy, S.

Edgerton, W.F., "The Government and the Governed in the Egyptian Empire," *JNES* 6, 1974, pp. 152-160.

Elat, M., "The Political Status of the Kingdom of Judah within the Assyrian Empire in the 7th Century B.C.E.," in Y. Aharoni *et al., Investigations at Lachish: The Sanctuary and the Residency (Lachish V),* Tel Aviv 1975, pp. 61-70.

Engnell, I., *A Rigid Scrutiny,* ed. by J.T. Willis, Nashville 1969.

——, *Studies in Divine Kingship in the Ancient Near East,* Uppsala 1943.

Eph'al, I., "'Arabs' in Babylonia in the Eight Century B.C.," *JAOS* 94/74, pp. 108-115.

Erman, A. and Grapow, H., *Wörterbuch der ägyptischen Sprache* I, Leipzig 1926.

Evenari, M., Shanan, L. and Tadmor, N., *The Negev. The Challenge of a Desert,* Cambridge, Mass., 1971.

Falkenstein, A., "La cité-temple sumérienne," *CHM* 1, 1954, pp. 784-814 (Engl. transl. by Maria de J. Ellis: *The Sumerian Temple City,* Sources and Monographs, Monographs in History. Ancient Near East 1/1, Los Angeles 1974).

Fargo, V.M., *Settlement in Southern Palestine during Early Bronze III* (Unpubl. Ph.D. dissertation, University of Chicago), Chicago 1979.

Faulkner, R.O., "The Teaching of Merikare," in *The Literature of Ancient Egypt,* ed. by W.K. Simpson, New Haven and London 1977, pp. 180-192.

Feigin, S.I., "The Origin of *'ELOH,* 'God' in Hebrew," *JNES* 3, 1944, pp. 259.

Finet, A., "La place du devin dans la société de Mari," *RAI* 14, Paris 1966, pp. 87-93.

Fisher, L.R., "The Temple Quarter," *JSS* 8, 1963, pp. 34-41.

Fohrer, G., *History of Israelite Religion* (transl. by D.E. Green), Nashville and New York 1972.

——, *Introduction to the Old Testament,* Nashville and New York 1968.

Fontinoy, C., "Les noms de lieux en *-ayin* dans la Bible," *UF* 3, 1971, pp. 33-40.

Frankena, R., "The Vassal Treaties of Esarhaddon and the Dating of Deuteronomy," *Oudtestamentische Studiën* 14, 1965, pp. 122-154.

Frankfort, H., "Town Planning in Ancient Mesopotamia," *The Town Planning Review* 21, 1950, pp. 98-115.

Fritz, V., "Die sogenannte Liste der besiegten Könige in Jos. 12," *ZDPV* 85, 1969, pp. 136-161.

——, *Tempel und Zelt. Studien zum Tempelbau in Israel un zu den Zeltheiligtum der Priesterschrift* (WMANT 47), Neukirchen 1977.

——, see Kempinski, A.

Fürst, J., *Hebräisches und chaldäisches Handwörterbuch zum Alten Testament,* Leipzig 1876.

Gallary, J.A., "Town Planning and Community Structure," *The Legacy of Sumer,* ed. by Denise Schmandt-Besserat (Bibliotheca Mesopotamica IV), Malibu 1976, pp. 69-77.

Galling, K. (ed.), *Biblisches Reallexikon,* 2nd ed., Tübingen 1977.

——, *Die Erwählungstraditionen Israels* (BZAW 38), Giessen 1928.

Gardiner, A.H., *Ancient Egyptian Onomastica* I, Oxford 1947.

——, "An Ancient Egyptian List of the Fortresses of Nubia," *JEA* 3, 1916, pp. 184-192.

——, "The Coronation of King Ḥaremḥab," *JEA* 39, 1953, pp. 13-31.

Garelli, P., "Les temples at le pouvoir royal en Assyrie du XIVᵉ au VIIIᵉ siècle," *Le Temple et le Culte* (RAI 20), Leiden 1975, pp. 116-124.

Gelb, I.J., "The Arua Institution," *RA* 66, 1972, pp. 1-32.

——, *Glossary of Old Akkadian* (Materials for the Assyrian Dictionary 3), Chicago 1975.

——, "Thoughts about Ibla: A Preliminary Evaluation, March 1977," *Syro-Mesopotamian Studies* 1, 1977, pp. 3-30.

Geraty, L.T., "The 1974 Season of Excavations at Tell Ḥesbân," *Annual of the Department of Antiquities* (Jordan), 20, 1975, pp. 47-56.

——, see Boraas, R.S.

Gošo, H., see Höfnor, M.

Gibson, J.C.L., *Textbook of Syrian Semitic Inscriptions* I-II, Oxford 1971-75.

Ginsberg, H.L., "Judah and the Transjordan States from 734 to 582 B.C.E.," *Alexander Marx Jubilee Volume,* New York 1950, pp. 437-368.

Giveon, R., "An Egyptian Official at Gezer," *IEJ* 22, 1972, pp. 143-144.

——, *The Impact of Egypt on Canaan* (Orbis Biblicus et Orientalis 20), Freiburg and Göttingen 1978.

Glueck, N., *Explorations in Eastern Palestine* AASOR 25-28), Cambridge, Mass., 1951.

Goedicke, H., *The Report of Wenamun* (The Johns Hopkins Near Eastern Studies), Baltimore and London 1975.

Görg, M., *Untersuchungen zur hieroglyphischen Wiedergabe palästinischer Ortsname* (Bonner Biblische Beiträge, N.S. 29), Bonn 1971.

Goetze, A., "The City Khalbi and the Khapiru People," *BASOR* 79, 1940, pp. 32-34.

——, *Hethiter, Churriter und Assyrer* (Instittutet for Sammenlignende Kulturforskning. Serie A: XVII), Oslo 1936.

——, "From the Instructions for the Commander of the Border Guards," *ANET,* pp. 210-211.

——, "Instructions for Temple Officials," *ANET,* pp. 207-210.

——, Rev. of H. Bozkurt, M. Çiğ, and H.G. Güterbock: Istanbul Arkeoloji Müzlerinde Bulunan Boğazköy Tableterinden Seçme Metinler, 1944, *JCS* 1, 1947, pp. 82-92.

———, see Bezold, C.

Grafman, R., "Nehemiah's 'Broad Wall'," *IEJ* 24, 1974, pp. 50-51.

Grapow, H., see Erman, A.

Gray, J., *I & II Kings*, 2nd ed., Philadelphia 1970.

Grayson, A.K., *Assyrian Royal Inscriptions* 2, Wiesbaden 1976.

———, "The Walters Art Gallery Sennacherib Inscription," *AfO* 20, 1964, pp. 83-96.

Green, A.R., "Israelite Influence at Shishak's Court?," *BASOR* 233, 1979, pp. 59-62.

Greenfield, J.C., "The Dialects of Early Aramaic," *JNES* 37, 1978, pp. 93-99.

———, "Some Glosses in the Keret Epic," *Eretz Israel* 9, 1969, pp. 60-65.

Gressmann, H., *Die älteste Geschichtsschreibung und Prophetie Israels von Samuel bis Amos und Hosea* (Schriften des Alten Testaments II:1), Göttingen 1921.

Gunneweg, A.H.J., *Leviten und Priester. Hauptlinien der Traditionsbildung und Geschichte des israelitisch-jüdischen Kultpersonals* (FRLANT 89), Göttingen 1965.

Gurney, O.R., *The Hittites*, London 1952.

Gyles, M.F., *Pharaonic Policies and Administration 663 to 323 B.C.*, Chapel Hill., N.C., 1959.

Güterbock, H.G., "The Deeds of Suppiluliuma as told by his son, Mursili II," *JCS* 10, 1956, pp. 41-68, 75-98, 107-130.

———, "The Hittite Temple According to Written Sources," *Le Temple et le Culte* (RAI 20), Leiden 1975, pp. 125-132.

Habachi, L., "Découverte d'un temple-fortresse de Ramsès II," *La Revue du Caire* 33, 1955, pp. 62-65.

Hallo, W.W., *Early Mesopotamian Royal Titles: A Philological and Historical Analysis* (American Oriental Series 43), New Haven 1957.

Hammond, M., *The City in the Ancient World* (assisted by L.J. Barton), Cambridge, Mass., 1972.

Hanson, P.D., "Prolegomena to the Study of Jewish Apocalyptic," *Magnalia Dei; The Mighty Acts of God.* Essays on the Bible and Archaeology in Memory of G. Ernest Wright, ed. by F.M. Cross, W.E. Lemke, and P.D. Miller, Garden City, N.Y., 1976, pp. 389-413.

Haran, M., "Studies in the Account of the Levitical Cities. II. Utopia and Historical Reality," *JBL* 80, 1961, pp. 156-165.

———, "A Temple at Dor," *IEJ* 27, 1977, pp. 12-15.

———, *Temples and Temple-Service in Ancient Israel. An Inquiry into the Character of Cult Phenomena and the Historical Setting of the Priestly School*, Oxford 1978.

———, "Zeḇaḥ hayyamîm," *VT* 19, 1969, pp. 11-22.

Har-el, M., "The Valley of the Craftsmen (ge' haḥarašim)," *PEQ* 109, 1977, pp. 75-86.

Harris, Z.S., *A Grammar of the Phoenician Language* (AOS 8), New Haven, Conn., 1936.

Harrison, R.K., *Old Testament Times*, Grand Rapids, Mich., 1970.

Hawkins, J.D. and Davies, A.M., "On the Problems of Karatepe: The Hieroglyphic Text," *Anatolian Studies* 28, 1978, pp. 103-119.

Hayes, W.C., "Egypt: Internal Affairs from Thutmosis I to the death of Amenophis III," *CAH* II:1, Cambridge 1973, pp. 313-416.

Heaton, E.W., *Solomon's New Men. The Emergence of Ancient Israel as a Nation*, New York 1974.

Helck, W., *Die Beziehungen Ägyptens zu Vorderasien im 3. und 2. Jahrtausend v. Chr.*, Wiesbaden 1971.

———, *Zur Verwaltung des Mittleren und Neuen Reichs* (Probleme der Ägyptologie 3), Leiden-Cologne 1958.

Held, M., "The Root *ZBL/SBL* in Akkadian, Ugaritic, and Biblical Hebrew," *JAOS* 88, 1968, pp. 90-96.

Helms, S., "Jawa Excavations 1974. A Preliminary Report," *Levant* 8, 1976, pp. 1-35.

———, "Jawa Excavations 1975: Third Preliminary Report," *Levant* 9, 1977, pp. 21-35.

Helzer, M., *The Rural Community in Ancient Ugarit*, Wiesbaden 1976.

Herr, L.G., *The Scripts of Ancient Northwest Semitic Seals*, Missoula, Mont., 1978.

Herzog, Z., Rainey, A.F., and Moshkovitz, Sh., "The Stratigraphy at Beer-Sheba and the Location of the Sanctuary," *BASOR* 225, 1977, pp. 49-58.

Hölscher, G., "Levi," in *Real-Encyclopädie der classischen Altertumswissenschaft* XII: 2, ed. by Pauly, A.F. von–Wissowa, G., Stuttgart 1925, cols. 2155-2208.

Höfner, M., "Die vorislamischen Religionen Arabiens," in H. Gese, M. Höfner, K. Rudolph, *Die Religionen Altsyriens, Altarabiens und der Mandäer* (Die Religionen der Menschheit 10/2), Stuttgart 1970, pp. 234-402.

Hogarth, D.G., "Egyptian Empire in Asia," *JEA* 1, 1914, pp. 9-17.

Holland, T.A., "A Study of Palestinian Iron Age Baked Clay Figurines, with Special Reference to Jerusalem: Cave 1," *Levant* 9, 1977, pp. 121-155.

Hooke, S.H. (ed.), *Myth, Ritual, and Kingship*, Oxford 1958.

Hooker, E.M., "The Significance of Numa's Religious Reform," *Numen* 10, 1963, pp. 87-132.

Hrouda, B., "Le mobilier du temple," *Le Temple et le Culte* (RAI 20), Leiden 1975, pp. 151-155.

Hvidberg, F.F., "The Canaanite Background of Gen. I-III," *VT* 10, 1960, pp. 285-294.

———, *Weeping and Laughter in the Old Testament*, Leiden and Copenhagen 1962.

Hylander, I., *Die literarische Samuel-Saul-Komplex (1. Sam. 1-15) traditionsgechichtlich untersucht*, Uppsala und Leipzig 1932.

Ibrahim, M., Sauer, J.A., and Yassine, K., "The East Jordan Valley Survey," *BASOR* 222, 1976, pp. 41-66.

James, F.W., *The Iron Age at Beth-Shan* (Museum Monographs), Philadelphia 1966.

Jankowska, N.B., "Communal Self-Government and the King of the State of Arrapha," *JESHO* 12, 1969, pp. 233-282.

Johnson, A.R., "Hebrew Conceptions of Kingship," in *Myth, Ritual, and Kingship*, ed. by S.H. Hooke, Oxford 1958, pp. 204-235.

Kapelrud, A.S., "Temple Building, a Task for Gods and Kings," *Orientalia* 32, 1963, pp. 56-62.

Kaplan, H. and J., "Jaffa," *Encyclopedia of Archaeological Excavations in the Holy Land* II, Jerusalem 1976, pp. 532-541.

Katzenstein, H.J., *The History of Tyre*, Jerusalem 1973.

Kaufman, S.A., "The Structure of the Deuteronomic Law," *Maarav* 1, 1979, pp. 105-158.

Kaufmann, Y., *The Religion of Israel* (transl. and abridged by M. Greenberg), Chicago 1960.

Kees, H., "Ägypten," *Kulturgeschichte des Alten Orients* I (Handbuch der Altertumswissenschaft III, 1.3.I), München 1933.

Kelso, J.L., see Albright, W.F.

Kemp, B.J., "Fortified Towns in Nubia," *Man, Settlement and Urbanism*, ed. by P. Ucko, R. Tringham and G.W. Dimbleby, Cambridge, Mass., 1972, pp. 651-656.

Kempinski, A., "Beth-Shean. Late Bronze and Iron Age Temples," *Encyclopedia of Archaeological Excavations in the Holy Land* I, Jerusalem 1975, pp. 213-215.

Kempinski, A., see Aharoni, Y.

Kempinski, A., and Fritz, V., "Excavations at Tel Masos (Khirbet et Meshâsh). Preliminary Report on the Third Season, 1975," *Tel Aviv* 4, 1977, pp. 136-158.

Kenyon, K.M., *Amorites and Canaanites* (The Schweich Lectures of the British Academy 1963), London 1966.
———, *Digging up Jerusalem,* New York and Washington 1974.
———, see Crowfoot, J.W.
King, L.W., *Babylonian Boundary-Stones and Memorial-Tablets in the British Museum,* London 1912.
Kirsten, E., *Die griechische Polis als historisch-geographisches Problem des Mittelmeerraumes* (Colloquium Geographicum, Band 5), Bonn 1956.
Kitchen, K.A., "Some New Light on the Asiatic Wars of Rameses II," *JEA* 50, 1964, pp. 47-70.
———, *The Third Intermediate Period in Egypt (1100–650 B.C.),* Warminster 1973.
Klengel, H., *Geschichte und Kultur Altsyriens,* Heidelberg 1967.
———. "Die Rolle der 'Ältesten' (LÚ^MEŠ ŠU.GI) im Kleinasien der Hethiterzeit," *ZfA* 57, 1965, pp. 223-236.
———, "Zu den *šībūtum* in altbabylonischer Zeit," *Orientalia* 29, 1960, pp. 375–375.
Knudtzon, J.A., *Die Tell el-Amarna Tafeln* II, bearbeitet von O. Weber und E. Ebeling, Aalen 1964.
Kraeling, C.H., and Adams, R.M. (eds.), *City Invincible* (A Symposium on Urbanization and Cultural Development in the Ancient Near East at the Oriental Institute of the University of Chicago, December 4-7, 1958), Chicago 1960.
Kramer, S.N., *Enmerkar and the Lord of Aratta,* Philadelphia 1952.
———, "Lamentation over the Destruction of Sumer and Ur," *The Ancient Near East* (Suppl. to ANET), 1969, pp. 175-183 (611-619).
———, "Sumerian Historiography," *IEJ* 3, 1953, pp. 217-232.
———, *The Sumerians. Their History, Culture and Character,* Chicago 1963.
Kupper, J.-R., "Roi et šakkanaku," *JCS* 21, 1976, pp. 123-125.
———, *Correspondance de Kibri-Dagan gouverneur de Terqa* (ARM III), Paris 1950.
Kuschke, A., "Der Tempel Salomos und der 'syrische Tempeltypus'," *BZAW* 105, Berlin 1967, pp. 124-132.
———, "Tempel," *Biblisches Reallexikon* II, ed. by K. Galling, Tübingen 1977, pp. 333-335.
Kutsch, E., "Die Wurzel עצר im Hebräischen," *VT* 2, 1952, pp. 57-69.
Lambert, W.G., rev. of F. Gössmann; Das Era Epos, 1956, *AfO* 18, 1957–58, pp. 395-401.
Lampl, P., *Cities and Planning in the Ancient Near East,* New York 1968.
Langdon, S., *Die neubabylonischen Königsinschriften* (VAB 4), Leipzig 1912.
Lapp, P.W., "The 1963 Excavations at Ta'annek," *BASOR* 173, 1964, pp. 4-44.
———, "Palestine in the Early Bronze Age," *Near Eastern Archaeology in the Twentieth Century,* ed. by J.A. Sanders, Garden City, N.Y., 1970, pp. 101-131.
———, "Tell er-Rumeith," *RB* 70, 1963, pp. 406-411.
———, "Tell er-Rumeith," *RB* 75, 1968, pp. 98-105.
———, *The Tale of the Tell,* ed. by N. Lapp, Pittsburg 1975.
Larsen, M. Trolle, "The City and its King. On the Old Assyrian Notion of Kingship," *Le palais et la royauté* (RAI 19), Paris 1974, pp. 285-300.
Leeuwen, C. van, "Sanchérib devant Jérusalem," *Oudtestamentische Studiën* 14, 1965, pp. 245-272.
Lemaire, A., *Inscriptions hébraïques,* Paris 1977.
———, "L'ostracon de Meṣad Ḥashavyahu (Yavne-Yam) replacé dans son contexte," *Semitica* 21, 1971, pp. 57-79.
Levine, B.A., "Notes on a Hebrew Ostracon from Arad," *IEJ* 19, 1969, pp. 49-51.

Levy, S. and Edelstein, G., "Cinq années de fouilles à Tell 'Amal (Nir David), *RB* 79, 1972, pp. 325-367.

Lidzbarski, M., *Ephemeris für semitische Epigraphik,* Giessen 1915.

Liere, W.J. van, "Capitals and Citadels of Bronze Age Syria in their Relationship to Land and Water," *Annales archéologiques de Syrie* 13, 1963, pp. 107-122.

Lindblom, J., *Israels religion i gammaltestamentlig tid,* 2d ed., Stockholm 1953.

——, *Prophecy in Ancient Israel,* Philadelphia 1962 (1965).,

Liver, J., "Korah, Dathan and Abiram," *Scripta Hierosolymitana* 8, 1961, pp. 189-217.

——, "The Wars of Mesha, King of Moab," *PEQ* 99, 1967, pp. 13-31.

Liverani, M., "Memorandum on the Approach to Historiographic Texts," *Orientalia* 42, 1973, pp. 178-194.

Livingstone, D., "Location of Biblical Bethel and Ai Reconsidered," *The Westminster Theological Journal* 33, 1970, pp. 20-44.

Lohfink, H., "Die Bundesurkunde des Königs Josias. Eine Frage an die Deuteronomium-forschung," *Biblica* 44, 1963, pp. 261-288, 461-498.

Luckenbill, D.D., *The Annals of Sennacherib* (OIP II), Chicago 1924.

Maag, V., "Erwägungen zur deuteronomischen Kultcentralisation," *VT* 6, 1956, pp. 10-18.

Macalister, R.A.S., *The Excavations of Gezer* I, London 1911.

——, see Bliss, F.J.

Maisler (Mazar), B., "Excavations at Tell Qasîle. Preliminary Report," *IEJ* 1, 1950-51, pp. 61-76, 125-140, 194-218.

Matthews, V.H., "Government Involvment in the Religion of the Mari Kingdom," *RA* 72, 1978, pp. 151-156.

Matthiae, P., *Ebla. An Empire Rediscovered,* Garden City, N.Y. 1981.

——, "Ebla in the Late Early Syrian Period: The Royal Palace and the State Archives," *BA* 39, 1976, pp. 94-113.

——, see Pettinato, G.

May, H.G., "The Hebrew Seals and the Status of Exiled Jehoiakin," *AJSL* 56, 1939, pp. 146-148.

Mayes, A.D.H., "The Rise of the Israelite Monarchy," *ZAW* 90, 1978, pp. 1-19.

Mazar, A., "Excavations at Tell Qasîle, 1973–1974 (Preliminary Report)," *IEJ* 25, 1975, pp. 77-88.

Mazar, B., "The Cities of the Priests and the Levites," *SVT* 7, 1960, pp. 193-205.

——, "The Sanctuary of Arad and the Family of Hobab the Kenite," *JNES* 24, 1965, pp. 297-303.

——, "מֵישָׁע," *Encyclopaedia Biblica* IV, Jerusalem 1962, cols. 921-925.

——, see Maisler, B.

Mazar, B., Biran, A., Dothan, M., Dunayevsky, I., "'Ein Gev: Excavations in 1961," *IEJ* 14, 1964, pp. 1-49.

McEvan, C.W., "The Syrian Expedition of the Oriental Institute of the University of Chicago," *AJA* 41, 1937, pp. 8-16.

McKenzie, D.A., "The Judge of Israel," *VT* 17, 1967, pp. 118-121.

Mendelsohn, I., "On Corvée Labor in Ancient Canaan and Israel," *BASOR* 167, 1962, pp. 31-35.

——, "Samuel's Denunciation of Kingship," *BASOR* 143, 1956, pp. 17-22.

Meshel, Z., "Did Yahweh have a Consort? The New Religious Inscriptions from the Sinai," *Biblical Archaeology Review* 5, 1979, pp. 24-35.

——, "Horvat Ritma – An Iron Age Fortress in the Negev Highlands," *Tel Aviv* 4, 1977, pp. 110-135.

——, "Kuntillet 'Ajrud. An Israelite Religious Center in Northern Sinai," *Expedition* 20:4, 1978, pp. 50-54.

Meshel, Z., and Meyer, C., "The name of God in the Wilderness of Zin," *BA* 39, 1976, pp. 6-10.

Mettinger, T.N.D., *King and Messiah* (Coniectanea Biblica. Old Testament Series 8), Lund 1971.

——, *Solomonic State Officials* (Coniectanea Biblica. Old Testament Series 5), Lund 1971.

Meyer, C., see Meshel, Z.

Milgrom, J., *Studies in Levitical Terminology* I, Berkely, Cal., 1970.

Millard, A.R., "Epigraphic Notes, Aramaic and Hebrew," *PEQ* 110, 1978, pp. 23-26.

Miller, J.M., "The Moabite Stone as a Memorial Stela," *PEQ* 106, 1974, pp. 9-18.

Miller, R., "Water Use in Syria and Palestine from the Neolithic to Bronze Age," *World Archaeology* 11, 1980, pp. 331-339.

Mittmann, S., "Ri. 1, 16f. und das Siedlungsgebeit der kenitischen Sippe Hobab," *ZDPV* 93, 1977, pp. 213-235.

Montgomery, J.A., and Gehman, H.S., *A Critical and Exegetical Commentary on the Books of Kings* (ICC), New York 1951.

Moortgat, A., *Altvorderasiatische Malerai,* Berlin 1959.

Moran, W.L. "A Kingdom of Priests," in *The Bible in Current Catholic Thought,* ed. by J.L. McKenzie, New York 1962, pp. 7-20.

Morenz, S., *Ägyptische Religion* (Die Religionen der Menschheit 8), Stuttgart 1960.

Moshkovitz, Sh., see Herzog, Z.

Mosis, R., *Untersuchungen zur Theologie des chronistischen Geschichtswerks* (Freiburger Theologische Studien 29), Freiburg-Basel-Wien 1973.

Motzki, H., "Ein Beitrag zum Problem des Stierkultes in der Religionsgeschichte Israels," *VT* 25, 1975, pp. 470-485.

Münderlein, G., גרן, *ThWAT* II (1974) 1977, cols. 69-70.

Munn-Rankin, J.M., "Diplomacy in Western Asia in the Early Second Millennium B.C.," *Iraq* 18, 1956, pp. 68-110.

Murnane, W.J., *Ancient Egyptian Coregencies* (SAOC 40), Chicago 1977.

Na'aman, N., "Sennacherib's 'Letter to God' on his Campaign to Judah," *BASOR* 214, 1974, pp. 25-39.

Naumann, R., *Architektur Kleinasiens von ihren Anfängen bis zum Ende der hethitischen Zeit,* Tübingen 1955.

Naveh, J., "A Hebrew Letter from the Seventh Century B.C.," *IEJ* 10, 1960, pp. 129-139.

——, "More Hebrew Inscriptions from Meṣad Ḥashavyahu," *IEJ* 12, 1962, pp. 27-32, 89-99.

Nicholson, E.W., *Deuteronomy and Tradition,* Oxford 1967.

Nielsen, E., "Political Conditions and Cultural Development in Israel and Judah during the Reign of Manasseh," *4th World Congress of Jewish Studies* I, Jerusalem 1967, pp. 103-106.

——, "Shechem. A Traditio-Historical Investigation, Copenhagen 1955.

Nilsson, M.P., *Griechische Feste von religiöser Bedeutung mit Ausschluss der Attischen,* Leipzig 1906.

Nöldecke, T., "Aramäische Inschriften," *ZfA* 21, 1908, pp. 375-388.

North, R., "Does Archaeology Prove Chronicles Sources?," *A Light Unto My Path,* ed. by H.N. Bream, R.D. Heim, C.A. Moore, Philadelphia 1973, pp. 375-401.

Noth, M., "The Background of Judges 17-18," in *Israel's Prophetic Heritage,* ed. by B.W. Anderson and W. Harrelson, New York 1962, pp. 68-85.

——, "Das deutsche evangelische Institut für Altertumswissenschaft des Heiligen Landes. Lehrkurs 1956," *ZDPV* 73, 1957, pp. 1-58.

——, *The History of Israel,* 2nd ed., New York and Evanston 1960.

——, *Die israelitischen Personennamen im Rahmen der gemeinsemitischen Namengebung*, Stuttgart 1928.

——, *Könige I. 1-16* (BK X:1), Neukirchen 1968.

——, "Zum Ursprung der phönikischen Küstenstädte," *Welt des Orients* 1, 1947, pp. 21-28.

——, "Die Wege der Pharaonenheere in Palästina und Syrien. Untersuchungen zu den hieroglyphischen Listen palästinischer und syrischer Städte," *ZDPV* 60, 1937, pp. 183-239 (*Aufsätze* I, pp. 3-44).

——, "Die Wege der Pharaonenheere in Palästina und Syrien. IV. Die Shoschenkliste," *ZDPV* 61, 1938, pp. 277-304 (*Aufsätze* II, pp. 73-93).

Nyberg, H.S., *Studien zum Hoseabuche* (Uppsala Universitets Årsskrift 1935:6), Uppsala 1935.

——, "Studien zum Religionskampf im Alten Testament," *ARW* 35, 1938, pp. 329-387.

O'Connell, K., Rose, D.G., and Toombs, L.E., "Tell el-Ḥesi," *IEJ* 27, 1977, pp. 246-250.

Oded, B. "Judah and the Exile," in *Israelite and Judean History*, ed. by J.H. Hayes and J.M. Miller, Philadelphia 1977, pp. 435-488.

Oesterley, W.O.E., and Robinson, Th.H., *Hebrew Religion. Its Origin and Development*, London 1930 (1952).

Olávarri, E., "Fouilles à 'Arô'er sur l'Arnon. Les niveaux du bronze intermédiaire," *RB* 76, 1969, pp. 230-259.

Olmstead, A.T., *History of Assyria*, Chicago 1923 (1960).

Oppenheim, A.L., *Ancient Mesopotamia. Portrait of a Dead Civilization*, Chicago and London 1964.

——, "The Archives of the Palace of Mari, II. A Review-Article," *JNES* 13, 1954, pp. 141-148.

——, "Bird's-Eye View of Mesopotamian Economic History," in *Trade and Market in the Early Empires*, ed. by K. Polanyi, C.M. Arensberg and H.W. Pearson, New York and London 1957 (1965), pp. 27-37.

——, "The Mesopotamian Temple," *BA* 7, 1944, pp. 54-63.

Otten, H., "Götterreisen. B. Nach hethitischen Texten," *Reallexikon der Assyriologie und vorderasiatischen Archäologie* III, Berlin 1969, p. 483.

Otto, E., *Ägypten. Der Weg des Pharaonenreiches*, Stuttgart 1953 (1958).

Ottosson, M., *Gilead. Tradition and History* (Coniectanea Biblica. Old Testament Series 3), Lund 1969.

——, "Tempel och Palats i Jerusalem och Beth Shan," *SEÅ* 41-42, 1976-77, pp. 166-178.

——, *Temples and Cult Places in Palestine* (Boreas 12), Uppsala 1980.

Otzen, B., *Israeliterne i Palaestina*, København 1977.

Pardee, D. "An Overview of Ancient Hebrew Epistolography," *JBL* 97, 1978, pp. 321-346.

——, "Letters from Tel Arad," *UF* 10, 1978, pp. 289-336.

Peckham, B., "Israel and Phoenicia," in *Magnalia Dei: The Mighty Acts of God*, ed. by F.M. Cross, W.E. Lemke and P.D. Miller, Garden City, N.Y., 1976, pp. 224-248.

Pedersen, J., *Israel* I-IV, London and Copenhagen 1940 (1953).

Peterson, J.L., *A Topographical Survey of the Levitical "Cities" of Joshua 21 and 1 Chronicles 6: Studies in Israelite Life and Religion* (Unpubl. Th.D. diss., Seabury Western Theol. Seminary), Evanston, Ill. 1979.

Petrie, F., *Tell el Hesy (Lachish)*, London 1891.

Pettinato, G., "The Royal Archives of Tell Mardikh-Ebla," *BA* 39, 1976, pp. 44-52.

——, "Testi cuneiformi del 3. millennio in paleo-cananeo rinvenuti nella campagna 1974 a Tell Mardīkh = Ebla," *Orientalia* 44, 1975, pp. 361-374.

——, see Canciani, F.

Pettinato, G., and Matthiae, P., "Aspetti amministrativi e topografici di Ebla nel III millennio Av. Cr.," *Rivista degli Studi Orientali* 50, 1976, pp. 1-30.

Preuss, H.D., *Verspottung fremder Religionen im Alten Testament* (BWANT 92), Stuttgart 1971.

Price, I.M., "Some Observations on the Financial Importance of the Temple in the First Dynasty of Babylon," *AJSL* 32, 1915-16, pp. 250-260.

Rainey, A.F., "Bethel is still Beitin," *The Westminster Theological Journal* 33, 1970, pp. 175-188.

——, "Compulsory Labor Gangs in Ancient Israel," *IEJ* 20, 1970, pp. 191-202.

——, "The Samaria Ostraca in the Light of Fresh Evidence," *PEQ* 99, 1967, pp. 32-41.

——, see Herzog, Z.

Redford, D.B., "Studies in Relations between Palestine and Egypt during the First Millennium B.C.," *Studies on the Ancient Palestinian World,* ed. by J.W. Wevers and D.B. Redford, Toronto 1972, pp. 141-156.

Reed, W.L., see Vinnett, F.V.

Ringgren, *Israelite Religion,* Philadelphia 1966.

Robinson, Th.H., see Oesterley, W.O.E.

Röllig, W., see Donner, H.

Rose, D.G., see O'Connell, K.

Rothenberg, B., *Were these King Solomon's Mines?,* New York 1972.

Rowe, A., *The Four Canaanite Temples of Beth Shan* II:1, Philadelphia 1939.

Rowley, H.H., "Hezekiah's Reform and Rebellion," *BJRL* 44, 1961–62, pp. 396-431.

——, *Worship in Israel,* Philadelphia 1967.

Rudolph, K., *Chronikbücher* (HAT 21), Tübingen 1955.

——, see Höfner, M.

Säve-Söderbergh, T., *Ägypten und Nubien. Ein Beitrag zur Geschichte altägyptischer Aussenpolitik,* Lund 1941.

——, *Pharaohs and Mortals* (transl. by R.E. Oldenburg), Indianapolis and New York 1961.

Saggs, H.W.F., *The Encounter with the Divine in Mesopotamia and Israel,* London 1978.

——, *The Greatness that was Babylon,* New York 1962.

——, "The Nimrud Letters, 1952 – Part I. The Ukin-Zer Rebellion and Related Texts," *Iraq* 17, 1955, pp. 21-58.

Sauer, J.A., "Hesban 1974. Area B and Square D 4," *Andrews University Seminary Studies* 14, 1976, pp. 29-62.

——, rev. of A.D. Tushingham; The Excavations at Dibon (Dhībân) in Moab, AASOR 40, in *Annual of the Department of Antiquities (Jordan),* 20, 1975, pp. 103-109.

——, see Ibrahim, M.

Scharff, A., *Der historische Abschnitt der Lehre für König Merikarê* (Sitzungsberichte der Bayerischen Akademie der Wissenschaften 8), 1936.

Schmid, H.H., *Der sogennante Jahwist. Beobachtungen und Fragen zur Pentateuch-forschung,* Zürich 1976.

Schmidt, L., *Menschlicher Erfolg und Jahwes Initiative* (WMANT 38), Neukirchen 1970.

Schneider, N., "Der šangû als Verwaltungsbehörde und Opfergabenspender im Reiche der dritten Dynastie von Ur," *JCS* 1, 1947, pp. 122-142.

Seebass, H., "Tradition und Interpretation bei Jehu ben Chanani und Ahia von Silo," *VT* 25, 1975, pp. 175-190.

Segert, S. "Die Sprache der moabitischen Königsinschrift," *Archiv Orientalní* 29, 1961, pp. 197-267.

Sellin, E., *Geschichte des israelitisch-jüdischen Volkes* I, Leipzig 1924.

Seltzer, R.M., *Jewish People, Jewish Thought. The Jewish Experience in History*, New York and London 1980.

Seux, M.-J., *Épithètes royales akkadiennes et sumériennes*, Paris 1967.

Shanan, L., see Evenari, M.

Shea, W.H., "The Date and Significance of the Samaria Ostraca," *IEJ* 27, 1977, pp. 16-27.

———. "The Inscribed Late Bronze Jar Handle from Tell Halif," *BASOR* 232, 1978, pp. 78-80.

Shiloh, Y., "Iron Age Sanctuaries and Cult Elements in Palestine," *Symposia*, ed. by F.M. Cross, Cambridge, Mass., 1979, pp. 147-157.

———, "The Four-Room House – Its Situation and Function in the Israelite City," *IEJ* 20, 1970, pp. 180-190.

Siebens, A.R., *L'origine du code deuteronomique*, Paris 1929.

Simons, J., *The Geographical and Topographical Texts of the Old Testament*, Leiden 1959.

———, *Handbook for the Study of Egyptian Topographical Lists Relating to Western Asia*, Leiden 1937.

———, "The Wall of Manasseh and the 'Mishneh' of Jerusalem," *Oudtestamentische Studiën* 7, 1950, pp. 179-200.

Sjöberg, Å.W., "Die göttliche Abstammung der sumerisch-babylonischen Herrscher," *Orientalia Suecana* 21, 1972, pp. 87-112.

Smith, M., *Palestinian Parties and Politics that Shaped the Old Testament*, New York and London 1971.

———, "The Veracity of Ezekiel, the Sins of Manasseh, and Jeremiah 44:18," *ZAW* 87, 1975, pp. 11-16.

Soden, W. von, *Akkadisches Handwörterbuch*, Wiesbaden 1959–1981.

Soggin, J.A., "The Period of the Judges and the Rise of the Monarchy," in *Israelite and Judean History*, ed. by J.H. Hayes and J.M. Miller, Philadelphia 1977, pp. 332-380.

Sollberger, E., "The Temple in Babylonia," *Le Temple et le Culte* (RAI 20), Leiden 1975, pp. 31-34.

Spencer, J.R., *The Levitical Cities: A Study of the Role and Function of the Levites in the History of Israel* (Unpubl. Ph.D. dissertation, University of Chicago), Chicago 1980.

Stadelmann, R., *Syrisch-palästinensische Gottheiten in Ägypten* (Probleme der Ägyptologie 15), Leiden 1967.

Starke, F., "Ḫalmašuit im Anitta-Text und die hethitische Ideologie vom Königtum," *ZfA* 69, 1979, pp. 47-120.

Stern, E., "Azekah," *EAEHL* I, Jerusalem 1975, pp. 141-143.

———, *Excavations at Tel Mevorakh 1973-1976. Part One: From the Iron Age to the Roman Period* (Qedem 9), Jerusalem 1978.

———, Rev. of A.D. Tushingham; The Excavations at Dibon (Dhībân) in Moab, (AASOR 40), in *IEJ* 25, 1975, pp. 179-181.

Stinespring, W.F., "Temple, Jerusalem," *IDB* IV, New York and Nasville 1962, pp. 534-560.

Strauss, H., *Untersuchungen zu den Überlieferungen der vorexilischen Leviten*, (diss.), Bonn 1960.

Sturtevant, E.H., *A Hittite Chrestomathy*, Philadelphia 1935.

Sukenik, E.L., *The Buildings at Samaria*, London 1942.

Tadmor, H, "The Campaign of Sargon II of Assur: A Chronological-Historical Study," *JCS* 12, 1958, pp. 22-40, 77-100.

——, "On the History of Samaria in the Biblical Period," *Eretz Shomron,* Jerusalem 1972 (Hebrew), pp. 67-74.

——, "Philistia under Assyrian Rule," *BA* 29, 1966, pp. 86-102.

Tadmor, N., see Evenari, M.

Talmon, S. "Divergencies in Calendar-Reckoning in Ephraim and Judah," *VT* 8, 1958, pp. 48-74.

——, "Synonymous Readings in the Textual Traditions of the Old Testament," *Scripta Hierosolymitana* 8, Jerusalem 1961, pp. 335-383.

Tambiah, S.J., *World Conquerer and World Renouncer* (Cambridge Studies in Anthropology 15), Cambridge 1976.

Thomas, D.W. (ed.), *Documents from Old Testament Times,* London 1958.

Thompson, H.O., *Mekal. The God of Beth-Shan,* Leiden 1970.

Thompson, Th.L., *The Historicity of the Patriarchal Narratives. The Quest for the Historical Abraham* (BZAW 133), Berlin 1974.

Thureau-Dangin, F., "Nouvelles lettres d'el-Amarna," *RA* 19, 1922, pp. 91-108.

Toombs, L.E., "Shechem: Problems of the Early Israelite Era," *Symposia,* ed. by F.M. Cross, Cambridge, Mass., 1979, pp. 69-83.

——, "The Stratigraphy at Tell Balaṭah," *ADAJ* 17, 1972, pp. 99-110.

——, "The Stratigraphy of Tell Balaṭah (Shechem)," *BASOR* 223, 1976, pp. 57-59.

——, see O'Connell, K.

Torzyner, H., *Lachish I: The Lachish Letters,* Oxford 1938.

Tringham, R., see Ucko, P.J.

Tufnell, O. *et al., Lachish III: The Iron Age,* London 1953.

Tur-Sinai, H., see Torzyner, H.

Tushingham, A.D., *The Excavations at Dibon (Dhībân) in Moab. The Third Campaign 1952–53* (AASOR 40), Cambridge, Mass., 1972.

——, "A Royal Israelite Seal(?) and the Royal Jar Handle Stamp," *BASOR* 201, 1971, pp. 23-35.

——, "The Western Hill under the Monarchy," *ZDPV* 95, 1979, pp. 39-55.

Ulrich, E.C., *The Qumran Text of Samuel and Josephus* (Harvard Semitic Monographs 19), Missoula, Mont., 1978.

Uphill, E., "The Concept of the Egyptian Palace as a 'Ruling Machine'," in *Man, Settlement, and Urbanism,* ed. by P.J. Ucko, R. Tringham, and G.W. Dimbleby, Cambridge, Mass., 1972, pp. 721-734.

Ussishkin, D., "Building IV in Hamath and the Temples of Solomon and Tell Tayanat," *IEJ* 16, 1966, pp. 104-110.

——, "King Solomon's Palaces," *BA* 36, 1973, pp. 78-105.

Van Seters, J., *Abraham in History and Tradition,* New Haven and London 1975.

Vanstiphout, H., "Political Ideology in Early Sumer," *Orientalia Lovaniensia Periodica* I, 1970, pp. 7-38.

Vaughan, P.H., *The Meaning of 'bāmâ' in the Old Testament* (Society for Old Testament Study. Monograph Series 3), Cambridge 1972.

Vaux, R. de, *Ancient Israel* I-II, New York and Toronto 1961 (1965).

——, "Le roi d'Israël, vassal de Yahwé," *Mélanges E. Tisserant* I (Studi e Testi 231), Rome 1964, pp. 119-133 (Engl. transl. in *The Bible and the Ancient Near East,* Garden City, N.Y., 1971, pp. 152-166).

——, "Titres et functionnaries égyptiens à la cour de David et Salomon," *RB* 48, 1939, pp. 394-405.

Viganò, L., *Nomi e titoli di YHWH alla luce del semitico del Nord-ovest* (Biblica et Orientalia 31), Rome 1976.

Vinnett, F.V., and Reed, W.L., *The Excavations at Dibon (Dhībân) in Moab. Part II: The Second Campaign, 1952* (AASOR 36-37), Cambridge, Mass., 1964.

Volten, A., *Zwei altägyptische politische Schriften. Die Lehre für König Merikarê (Pap. Carlsberg VI) und die Lehre des Königs Amenemhet*, Kφbenhavn 1945.

Wachtsmuth, F., *Der Raum* I, Marburg 1929.

Wallis, G., "Jerusalem und Samaria als Königsstädte," *VT* 26, 1976, pp. 480-496.

Ward, W.A., "Egypt and the East Mediterranean in the Early Second Millennium B.C.," *Orientalia* 30, 1961, pp. 22-45, 129-155.

——, "The Egyptian Office of Joseph," *JSS* 5, 1960, pp. 144-150.

Waters, K.H., *Herodotus on Tyrants and Despots. A Study in Objectivity* (Historia. Zeitschrift für die alte Geschichte, Einzelschriften, Heft 15), Wiesbaden 1971.

Weber, O., see Knudtzon, J.A.

Weidner, E., "Hof- und Harems-Erlasse assyrischer Könige aus dem 2. Jahrtausend v. Chr.," *AfO* 17, 1954-56, pp. 257-293.

Weinberg, P., "Die Agrarverhältnisse in der Bürger-Tempel-Gemeinde der Achämenidenzeit," *Acta Antiqua* 22, 1974, pp. 473-486.

Weinfeld, M., *Deuteronomy and the Deuteronomic School*, Oxford 1972.

——, "Cult Centralization in Israel in the Light of a Neo-Babylonian Analogy," *JNES* 23, 1964, pp. 202-212.

Weippert, M., "Zum Präskript der hebräischen Briefe von Arad," *VT* 25, 1975, pp. 202-212.

——, *The Settlement of the Israelite Tribes in Palestine* (transl. by J.D. Martin, Studies in Biblical Theology, Sec. Ser. 21), Naperville, Ill. 1971.

——, "Elemente phönikischer und kilikischer Religion in den Inschriften vom Karatepe", *XVII. Deutscher Orientalistentag vom 21. bis 27. Juli 1968 in Würzburg, Vorträge* I (Supplementa I, ZDMG), Wiesbaden 1969, pp. 191-217.

Weiser, A., "Samuels 'Philister-Sieg'. Die Überlieferungen in 1. Samuel 7," *ZThK* 56, 1959, pp. 253-272.

——, *Samuel. Seine geschichtliche Aufgabe und religiöse Bedeutung* (FRLANT 81), Göttingen 1962.

Wellhausen, J., *Prolegomena to the History of Ancient Israel with a Reprint of the Article Israel from the Encyclopaedia Britannica* (A Meridian Book), Cleveland and New York 1957 (1961).

Welten, P., *Geschichte und Geschichtsdarstellung in den Chronikbüchern* (WMANT 42), Neukirchen 1973.

Widengren, G., *Religionsphänomenologie,* Berlin 1969.

——, *Sakrales Königtum im Alten Testament und im Judentum* (Franz Delitzsch-Vorlesungen 1952), Stuttgart 1955.

——, "What do we know about Moses?," in *Proclamation and Presence*, ed. by J.I. Durham and J.R. Porter, Richmond, Virginia 1970, pp. 21-47.

Wildberger, H., "Die Rede des Rabsake vor Jerusalem," *ThZ* 35, 1979, pp. 35-47.

Williams, R.J., "A People Come out of Egypt. An Egyptologist looks at the Old Testament," *SVT* 28, Leiden 1975, pp. 231-252.

Wilson, J.A., "Egyptian Instructions," *ANET,* pp. 412-425.

——, "The Function of the State," in *Before Philosophy*, ed. by H. and H.A. Frankfort, J.A. Wilson and T. Jacobsen, Chicago 1946 (1972), pp. 71-103.

——, "The Journey of Wen-Amon to Phoenicia," *ANET,* pp. 25-29.

Wiseman, D.J., *The Alalakh Tablets* (Occasional Publications of the British Institute of Archaeology at Ankara 2), London 1953.

Wolley, L., and Barnett, R.D., *Carchemish III. The Excavations in the inner Town and the Hittite Inscriptions,* London 1952.

Wokalek, A., *Griechische Stadtbefestigungen. Studien zur Geschichte der frühgriechischen Befestigungsanlagen* (Abhandlungen zur Kunst-, Musik- und Literaturwissenschaft, Band 136), Bonn 1973.

Wolff, H.W., *Dodekapropheton 1. Hosea,* Neukirchen 1961.

———, *Dodekapropheton 2. Joel und Amos,* Neukirchen 1969.

Wright, G.E., "The Levites in Deuteronomy," *VT* 4, 1954, pp. 325-330.

———, "The Provinces of Solomon," *Eretz Israel* 8, 1967, pp. 58*-68*.

———, *Shechem. The Biography of a Biblical City,* New York and Toronto 1965.

———, "Shechem," *EAEHL* IV, Jerusalem 1978, pp. 1083-1094.

Yadin, Y. "Beer-sheba: The High Place Destroyed by King Josiah," *BASOR* 222, 1976, pp. 5-17.

———, "Four Epigraphical Queries," *IEJ* 24, 1974, pp. 30-36.

———, *Hazor. The Head of All Those Kingdoms, Joshua 11:10* (The Schweich Lectures of the British Academy 1970), London 1972.

———, "A Note on the Stratigraphy of Arad," *IEJ* 15, 1965, p. 180.

Yaron, R., *The Laws of Eshnunna,* Jerusalem 1969.

Yassine, K., see Ibrahim, M.

Yeivin, S., "Did the Kingdoms of Israel have a Maritime Policy?," *JQR* 50, 1959–1960, pp. 193-228.

———, "On the Use and Misuse of Archaeology in Interpreting the Bible," *American Academy for Jewish Research, Proceedings* 34, 1966, pp. 141-154.

Yeivin, Z., "Es-Samo'a (As-Samu')," *IEJ* 21, 1971, pp. 74-75.

Zabłocka, J., "Palast und König. Ein Beitrag zu den neuassyrischen Eigentumsverhältnissen," *Altorientalische Forschungen* 1 (Schriften zur Geschichte und Kultur des Alten Orients 11), 1974, pp. 91-113.

Zijl, A.H. van, *The Moabites,* Leiden 1960.

Zimmerli, W., *Ezechiel* (BK XIII), Neukirchen 1969.

INDEX OF PASSAGES

INDEX OF TOPICS AND NAMES

INDEX OF AUTHORS